THE CONTEMPLATIVE PRACTITIONER

Meditation in Education and the Workplace

Second Edition

Meditation is a simple and practical activity that can enrich our lives and work in innumerable ways. It allows us to connect more deeply to ourselves and others and to the natural environment. In this book, John P. Miller, an expert in the field of holistic education, looks at meditation and how it can be integrated into one's work and daily life.

Twenty years after it was first published, Miller's book remains one of the best guides to contemplative practice, covering a variety of theoretical, empirical, historical, and cross-cultural approaches. For this new edition, Miller has updated the text to reflect the growth of the mindfulness movement, new research on the brain, and his years of experience teaching and practising contemplation in teacher education.

Whether one is interested in exploring how meditation can be used in the classroom or the workplace, or simply seeking to integrate it into one's personal life, *The Contemplative Practitioner* is the perfect companion.

JOHN P. MILLER is a professor in the Department of Curriculum, Teaching, and Learning at the Ontario Institute for Studies in Education, University of Toronto. He is the author or editor of 17 books on holistic learning and contemplative practices in education.

JOHN P. MILLER

The Contemplative Practitioner

Meditation in Education and the Workplace

Second Edition

UNIVERSITY OF TORONTO PRESS
Toronto Buffalo London

© University of Toronto Press 2014
Toronto Buffalo London
www.utppublishing.com
Printed in Canada
First published in 1994 by Bergin and Garvey, an imprint of ABC-CLIO, LLC;
paperback edition published in 1996 by OISE Press.

ISBN 978-1-4426-4742-8 (cloth)
ISBN 978-1-4426-1553-3 (paper)

∞

Printed on acid-free, 100% post-consumer recycled paper with vegetable-based inks.

Library and Archives Canada Cataloguing in Publication

Miller, John P., 1943–, author
The contemplative practitioner : meditation in education
and the workplace / John P. Miller. – Second edition.

Includes bibliographical references and index.
ISBN 978-1-4426-4742-8 (bound). – ISBN 978-1-4426-1553-3 (pbk.)

1. Meditation.   2. Contemplation.   3. Educators – Religious life.
4. College students – Religious life.   5. Miller, John P., 1943–.   I. Title.

BL627.M54 2013   204'.35   C2013-905640-8

University of Toronto Press acknowledges the financial assistance to its publishing
program of the Canada Council for the Arts and the Ontario Arts Council.

  Canada Council   Conseil des Arts
for the Arts   du Canada

University of Toronto Press acknowledges the financial support of the Government of
Canada through the Canada Book Fund for its publishing activities.

Chapter 2 was adapted from John P. Miller with Susan Drake,
"Beyond Reflection to Being: The Contemplative Practitioner,"
in *Phenomenology and Pedagogy* 9(1991):319–334.

Selected excerpts from Lao-tzu, *Tao Te Ching*, trans. Stephen Mitchell
(New York: HarperCollins 1988),
are reprinted by permission of HarperCollins.

The first part of chapter 7 was previously published in *Spirituality in Social Work
and Education: Theory, Practice, and Pedagogies*, ed. Janet Groen, Diana Coholic,
and John R. Graham (Wilfrid Laurier Press 2012), 187–204.

Contents

Foreword

You have in your hands an introduction to a set of practices and a way of being that many of us are seeking as our lives become more fragmented, our attention drawn to one screen or decision after another, and our very earth threatened by ever-new challenges. Not only is this an introduction to contemplative methods for bringing a centred, clear insight and a kind heart to each moment but it is also, and most unusual, a guide to bringing contemplative awareness into our work in the world, from education to a range of other professions.

Contemplative practices come from traditions all over the world. Examples include various forms of meditation, time in nature, writing, contemplative arts, and contemplative movement, including yoga. They cultivate a critical, first-person focus, sometimes with direct experience as the object, at other times concentrating on complex ideas or situations. Contemplative methods incorporated into daily life connect us to what we find most meaningful as they help us quiet our minds in the midst of action and distraction. Recent research has shown that contemplative practices can reduce stress and enhance creativity as well as develop capacities for deep concentration, greater empathy, communication, and improved focus and attention.

In recent years at the Center for Contemplative Mind in Society, we have seen these practices result in changes in how people make their living as well as how they live. Engineers at Google, trained in mindfulness, listen more fully to each other and discover more creative uses of their technology. University professors, in disciplines from physics to poetry, guide their students in a new kind of understanding, linking the external subject matter to their inner lives. Lawyers learn that seeing things just as they are in the present helps them move towards a more just outcome for the future. Practice has helped people be more compassionate, kinder, more thoughtful, and more honest.

Jack Miller is a great guide to this world of awakening. When we started the Center, his was the only book I could find on bringing contemplative awareness into the professions. Now that many people have explored the benefits of integrating ancient wisdom practices into contemporary life with its peculiar challenges, he has enriched that pioneering guide with the insight gained through these years of witnessing others and practising himself. Regardless of what role you may play in the world, you will learn a way of being from this book that is likely to make you happier in doing it. May you enjoy the book, the practices, and your life.

Mirabai Bush
Founder and Senior Fellow of the Center
for Contemplative Mind in Society

Acknowledgments

I am very grateful to the University of Toronto Press for undertaking another one of my books. Doug Hildebrand has been particularly helpful. His encouragement and the guidance of the review and acquisition process has been excellent. The comments of the three blind reviewers were very helpful. They made initial comments on the proposal and made suggestions about revisions of the complete manuscript. Thanks again to Anne Laughlin for overseeing the production process of one of my books. I never fail to be amazed by copyediting work, which requires such attention to detail. Thank you, Kate Baltais, for your careful editing of the text.

For years I have admired the work that Mirabai Bush has done at the Center for Contemplative Mind in Society and was delighted when she agreed to write the forward. Thank you, Mirabai, for writing such a thoughtful introduction to this book.

This year I received recognition from both the University of Toronto and the Ontario Institute of Studies in Education for my forty years of service. This book would not have been possible without the students with whom I have worked for all those years in the Department of Curriculum, Teaching, and Learning at the Ontario Institute for Studies in Education at the University of Toronto. Several students have contributed material to this book; so many others, who are not named, through their enthusiastic participation in my classes continually renew my energy and commitment to work described here. The help of my colleagues at OISE has also been invaluable; the work described in the last chapter would not have been possible without their support.

Finally, I thank my wife, Midori, who proofread the first draft of this book and has said that *The Contemplative Practitioner* is her personal favourite of the books I have written.

THE CONTEMPLATIVE PRACTITIONER

Meditation in Education and the Workplace

Second Edition

Chapter One

The Contemplative Practitioner

Contemplation seems alien to modern life. Our life today tends to be hurried and task oriented. We often find that each day we have a long list of things to do with little time to do them. The demands just to keep up can be overwhelming.

In contrast, contemplation is not task oriented. Although there are long-term expectations, normally contemplation is not practised to achieve something immediate. With so much to do, simply sitting still seems counter to the whole direction of modern life. Yet, despite this apparent incongruity, many people who undertake some form of contemplative practice find it healing.

I have introduced meditation to approximately two thousand students where I teach at the Ontario Institute for Studies in Education, which is part of the University of Toronto. Most of my students are teachers pursuing a graduate degree, but I also teach students in our Initial Teacher Education. I write about my experiences in the last chapter, but let me say here that I have witnessed many small miracles that have occurred as result of contemplative practices. Some of my students find they have more restful sleep, others report it makes them less reactive when a student acts out in the classroom, but most simply find that contemplative practice brings more serenity into their lives. Thus, what seems so alien to modern life may be profoundly healing. As life speeds up, we feel the need to slow down. As we are constantly confronted with external stimuli, we find that we need to turn inward. As we are called on to be more linear and rational, we find that the intuitive response is sometimes more appropriate. As the noise increases, silence beckons. With the pressure to stay connected to the Internet and email, there can also be a longing to connect to our souls, to others in an embodied way, to the earth, and to the cosmos.

What Is Contemplation?

Contemplation involves attention and awareness. Today, our attention is pulled in a multitude of directions through technology and the media. We seem to rarely experience what Jiddu Krishnamurti (1969) is referring to in telling us, "When you look totally you will give your whole attention, your whole being, everything of yourself, your eyes, your ears, your nerves. You will attend with complete self-abandonment" (31).

When we attend to the world in the manner suggested by Krishnamurti, we begin to see and relate to our environment in a different way. In fragmented consciousness, we are pushed and pulled by the outside world; from contemplative awareness, we see things as they are in the here and now. This type of awareness has also been called the "flow experience" (Csikszentmihalyi and Csikszentmihalyi 1988). The flow experience is where we lose, temporarily, the awareness of our separate self (e.g., the ego) and become totally focused on what we are doing. Mihaly Csikszentmihalyi (1988) cites research that indicates that this state is an optimal state for performing any task. In other words, when we are deeply attentive, we are most likely to enjoy our work and do it well. The research on the flow experience shows one important link between contemplation and daily life. Contemplation can help us experience the flow state more often and as a result more fully participate in our work.

When we are fully attentive we also may experience a sense of the sacred. For example, Csikszentmihalyi (1988) notes:

> The climber feels at one with the mountain, the clouds, the rays of the sun, and the tiny bugs moving and out of the shadow of the fingers holding to the rock; the surgeon feels at one with the movements of the operating team, sharing the beauty and the power of a harmonious transpersonal system. (33)

When we experience the sacred moment, we don't need anything else. The experience is satisfying in and of itself, as we are not doing something to get something else. As a result, we become totally attuned to what is happening in the moment.

Thomas Merton (1972) describes the sacred nature of contemplation like this:

> Contemplation is the highest expression of man's intellectual and spiritual life. It is that life itself, fully awake, fully active, fully aware that it is alive. It

is spiritual wonder. It is spontaneous awe at the sacredness of life, of being. It is gratitude for life, for awareness and for being. It is a vivid realization of the fact that life and being in us proceed from an invisible, transcendent, and infinitely abundant Source. (1)

Contemplation is characterized by a radical openness where the individual does not try to control what is happening. In the words of Brother David Steindl-Rast:

Then there comes a higher stage called "contemplation," where you are no longer in control of the process. Instead, you open yourself, you drop the word or passage or the image you've been dealing with, and you're just *there*. (Cited in Bodian 1985, 28; original emphasis)

Merton and Steindl-Rast come from the Christian tradition. Zia Inayat-Khan (2011) presents the Islamic perspective, where "contemplation (*muraqaba*) refers to the process of deepening reflection while meditation (*mushahada*) refers to awareness without thought content." (97). In Buddhism, meditation as a term is used more frequently than contemplation. Meditation seeks to cultivate what Shunryu Suzuki Roshi (1970) calls "beginner's mind" where we see directly into the nature of things:

For Zen students the most important thing is not to be dualistic. Our "original mind" includes everything within itself. It is always rich and sufficient within itself. You should not lose your self-sufficient mind. This does not mean a closed mind, but actually an empty mind and a ready mind. If your mind is empty, it is always ready for anything; it is open to everything. In the beginner's mind there are many possibilities; in the expert's mind there are few ... The beginner's mind is the mind of compassion. When our mind is compassionate, it is boundless. (21–2)

The ultimate goal of meditation in Buddhism is the development of wisdom and compassion. Robert Thurman (2011) explains, "Wisdom (*prajna*) is not accumulated instrumental knowledge, but is rather a special kind of super-knowing, a knowing by becoming the known, by transcending the subject-object duality" (27).

In this book, *contemplation is conceived as non-dualistic experience where we become one with what we are observing*. For example, in reflection, we think *about* something while in contemplation we tend to merge with the object. Examples of contemplation are included in the next chapter, where I also discuss the distinction between reflection and contemplation in more detail. Sometimes contemplation can lead to a sense of awe and wonder.

Meditation is one form of contemplation, which involves concentrated practice. Meditation is broadly conceived here as a contemplative practice and includes many types, such as *vipassana* (or insight meditation), visualization, and mantra. Contemplation can also include spontaneous and unstructured moments where we experience being fully present. Susan Smalley and Diana Winston (2010) describe some of these experiences:

> Maybe you have this sense in the midst of creative endeavors, like painting, writing, or making music. Maybe it happens when you are running that second mile, when you are cycling or during a pickup basketball game. Maybe this is the sense you had when you fell in love and it seemed as if only the two of you existed on the planet. Maybe it accompanied the birth of your child or came to you while taking a walk and holding a grandchild's hand. (11)

Smalley and Winston suggest that most of us have these kinds of experiences. Contemplative practitioners create the possibility for more of these moments to arise. As much as possible in a hectic and frantic world, they try to live contemplatively. This means living more in the moment and not in the past or future. It also means living more compassionately, as they see the intimate connections to others, the earth, and the universe.

Rationale for Contemplation/Meditation

Since the first edition of this book, a substantial amount of research on the effects of meditation practice has been published. Smalley and Winston (2010, xvii) summarize the benefits of mindfulness meditation in:

- Reducing stress
- Reducing chronic physical pain
- Boosting the body's immune system to fight disease
- Coping with painful life events, such as the death of a loved one or major illness
- Dealing with negative emotions like anger, fear, and greed
- Increasing self-awareness to detect harmful reactive patterns of thought, feeling, and action
- Improving attention or concentration

- Enhancing positive emotions, including happiness and compassion
- Increasing interpersonal relationships
- Reducing addictive behaviours, such as eating disorders, alcoholism, and smoking
- Enhancing performance, whether in work, sports, or academics
- Stimulating and releasing creativity
- Changing positively the actual structure of our brains.

A detailed examination of some of this research can be found in chapters 3 and 6 of this book. Given this research, why don't more people practise meditation? Generally, our society has surrounded meditation with a lot of psychological baggage. For example, religious fundamentalists link meditation with the occult. Others view meditation as something silly.

Besides the empirical research, there are other reasons for practising meditation. Contemplation allows the individual to gradually overcome his or her sense of separateness. Our society reinforces the personal ego, which spends most of the day planning, striving, and competing. Our ego arises from the various social roles we engage in such as parent, worker, and spouse. To the extent that we identify with these roles is also the extent of our suffering. For example, if people invest their whole identity in their work (e.g., the workaholic), they may find it extremely difficult to adjust when they retire. The father who is too attached to his role as father may have a difficult time of letting go of his son or daughter when he or she leaves home. Almost every spiritual tradition focuses on letting go of our ego and letting our original self arise.

I like Ralph Waldo Emerson's conception of the ego and this original self about which he wrote in his journal:

> A man finds out that there is somewhat in him that knows more than he does. Then he comes presently to the curious question, Who's who? which of these two is really me? the one that knows more or the one that knows less; the little fellow or the big fellow? (1909–14, vol. 9, 190)

The little fellow is our ego, which tries to manipulate the universe according to its own ends, while the big fellow is our original self and is in accord with the harmony of things. Gabriel Marcel has said the deeper we go within ourselves, the more we find that which is beyond ourselves.

The social structure we live in continually reinforces the ego through competition and fear. Thus, we constantly are trying to gain an edge on others in our work, on the highway, or when we stand in line at the post office or the grocery store. Meditation lets us witness the striving of the ego. During meditation practice, we compassionately witness all our thoughts and ego trips, and very gradually, we begin to see that our fundamental identity is not the thoughts that form our ego structure, but that clear awareness that is witnessing the arising and falling of all this stuff. This basic insight is the beginning of liberation and compassion.

The Power of Presence

In meditation, we work to be present to what is happening in the moment. Thus we cultivate the quality of presence. I like Debbie Hall's (2007) description of this quality:

I BELIEVE IN THE POWER OF PRESENCE.

I was recently reminded of this belief when I and several other Red Cross volunteers met a group of evacuees from Hurricane Katrina. We were there, as mental health professionals, to offer "psychological first aid." Despite all the training in how to "debrief," to educate about stress reactions, and to screen for those needing therapy, I was struck again by the simple healing power of presence. Even as we walked in the gate to the shelter, we were greeted with a burst of gratitude from the first person we encountered. I felt appreciated, but somewhat guilty, because I hadn't really done anything yet.

Presence is a noun, not a verb; it is a state of being, not doing. States of being are not highly valued in a culture that places a high priority on doing. Yet, true presence or "being with" another person carries with it a silent power – to bear witness to a passage, to help one carry an emotional burden, or to begin a healing process. In it, there is an intimate connection with another that is perhaps too seldom felt in a society that strives for ever-faster "connectivity."

... With therapy clients, I am still pulled by the need to do more than be, yet repeatedly struck by the healing power of connection created by being fully there in the quiet understanding of another. I believe in the power of presence, and it is not only something we give to others. It always changes me and always for the better. (100–2)

This power of presence is critical to all relationship, yet it is sometimes hard to find in our hurried lives. Our minds are filled with thoughts, worries, and plans that are barriers to presence.

John O'Donohue (1999) writes about presence:

Presence is the whole atmosphere of a person or thing ... Presence has a depth that lives behind the form or below the surface. There is a well of presence within every thing, but it is usually hidden from the human eye. This comes in different ripples to the surface. No two states of presence are every exactly the same. The flow of soul within means the surface is always different. (53–4)

Although attentiveness is at the core of presence, there is also a mysterious element – soul. O'Donohue talks about charismatic presence which is rooted in self-belonging. He writes, "It is the art of belonging to one's soul that keeps one's presence aflame" (66). O'Donohue believes this anchoring of presence in soul leads to dignity and beauty. With this dignity, there is "no forcing of presence," these people "do not drive themselves outwards to impress" (68). So, for O'Donohue, there is a quality of mystery to presence. Certainly, in people like Nelson Mandela we can sense a strong soulful presence. It is my belief, from working with meditation and introducing it to students, that meditation nourishes the soul and enhances our presence (Miller 2000).

Avraham Cohen (2009) has this to say about presence:

Presence involves listening not only with ears and mind but also listening with heart, which means hearing the emotions and the essence of the persons who speak, *hearing* what is not said, and hearing those who do not speak overtly, and listening for what is in the quietness. (46, original emphasis)

For Cohen, "presence is equivalent to love. Giving full presence to another is, I believe, the greatest gift a person can offer" (38).

Eckhart Tolle writes about presence in *The New Earth: Awakening to Your Life's Purpose* (2005): "Alert attention is Presence ... Being present is always infinitely more powerful than anything one could say or do, although sometimes being present can give rise to words or actions" (84, 176). For Tolle, Presence frees us from ego as it brings us into the now. Tolle, recalling ancient wisdom, refers to the Whole. Presence brings us into harmony with the Whole or the cosmos: "the whole comprises all that exists. It is the world or the cosmos. But all things in existence, from microbes to human beings to galaxies, are not really separate things or entities, but form part of a web of interconnected multidimensional processes" (275–6). Within the Whole is a "hidden harmony" where everything has a "perfect place" (195). Being present allows us access to this harmony. Tolle's view of the Whole echoes Marcus Aurelius, who states in *Meditations* (1997), "This you must always bear in mind, what is the nature of the whole, and what is my nature, and how this is related to that" (9).

Peter Senge, Otto Sharmer, Joseph Jaworski, and Betty Sue Flowers (2004) have developed the concept of presence in the context of organizations, and they see presence as deep listening as well as letting go of old identities and the need to control. Presence is a "letting come," which involves "consciously participating in a larger field of change" (14). They suggest that change in an organization can be seen as a U, which includes three steps – *sensing, presencing,* and *realizing. Sensing* is at the top of the U and involves observing and listening without preconceptions. Here there is an allowing to become "one with the situation" (88). *Presencing* is at the bottom of the U and involves connecting what we see in the sensing stage to the emerging whole. Here the people in the organization do not act out of ego but from the unconditioned self that is connected to the larger purpose of the organization: "We chose the term 'presencing' to describe this sate because it is about becoming totally present – to the larger space or field around us, to an expanded sense of self, and, ultimately, to what is emerging through us" (91). Moving up the right side of the U is *realizing* where people begin to act in accordance with emerging vision. People do not feel alone but connected to others and participate in "cocreation." There is not a sense of "I" or "We" are doing something, but the "experience is one of unbroken awareness and action" (92). Senge and his colleagues refer to the invisible world and make reference to the work of Christopher Bache, which is discussed in chapter 5. At the end of their book, Otto Scharmer tells us, "For me, the core of presencing is waking up together – waking up to who we really are by linking with and acting from our highest future Self – and by using the Self as a vehicle for bringing forth new worlds" (234). Senge and his associates discuss contemplative work not as an individual act, but one that is collective.

Presence in the Classroom

In my classes, I have had many students bring mindful presence into their teaching. A student in my class who teaches in elementary school, Rebecca

Ross-Zainotz (2012), worked on being more present to a very difficult student in her class. This boy was constantly seeking attention through negative behaviour towards other students. The student's behaviour was beginning to affect the whole class and the teacher's well-being. So, Rebecca decided to be more present to the student:

> I decided that in any interaction I had with the student, I would strive to be mindful. I made sure that I was aware and present when I was speaking with him. My body language was attentive and understanding. I made sure that when I was working with him and helping him one-on-one, I made eye contact and was focusing intently on listening to what he was saying. As he was writing a story about how an animal adapts to its habitat, I could tell he was appreciative of the change; the full attention that I was giving him at that moment. I continued with this approach in my interactions with him. When he would approach me with a question, or he would raise his hand on the carpet (without interrupting others), I made sure that I was present and aware of him and his request or response at that point in time.
>
> I gave him lots of opportunities to get my positive attention. I wanted him to realize that, when he was doing something positive, he got my positive energy and he got my attention more efficiently and consistently. I wanted him to want to do things that would catch my attention positively so that he would move away from any negative attention that he also may have wanted from me. Every opportunity in which he did something positive, or he was showing a positive attitude. I made sure to, in my mind, think: "I am present in this moment," and acknowledge this. Whether it was him getting out a pencil to complete a task, coming to the carpet on-time, or raising his hand before speaking, I was there, I was present and I made sure that I acknowledged this effort from him. (5–6)

When the student showed negative behaviour, Rebecca tried to not let this behaviour affect her approach:

> There were times, where I had to talk myself through the exercise, and breathe, in order to make sure my mood was not affected, or take a movement break, and speak to another student, but I made sure to focus on being aware of how his behaviour was affecting me, and I did my best to not let the negative energy become dominant in me. In these situations, I was very mindful of the words that I used around him, ensuring that they were always positive, and that I would not engage in a power struggle with him. (6–7)

Rebecca felt the whole experience of bringing mindfulness into her teaching was "powerful and moving." She found that the behaviour of the student became more positive:

> He seemed to be more understanding of situations where I was helping oth-er students, and not just him (as he would often previously get very upset if I wasn't giving him all my attention). We have now developed a relationship where he knows he will get quality, focused time in which I will help him. I became more consistent with my attentiveness toward him, dealt with him in a mindful manner and his behaviour adjusted.
>
> There are always going to be hard days, and days in which it is hard for him to move past his negative feelings about an issue at school, but on the whole, I feel like he trusts in the fact that I will give him the full attention and positive energy he deserves each day and that this will allow him to be successful. (Personal communication, 2012)

She also found that benefits of mindfulness impacted her life beyond the classroom:

> I realized that, personally, I have the ability to "take in" and embrace the world around me without "rushing through it," and that interactions with people, especially, those that need us the most, are extremely important to be present in – strangely and unexpectedly, more important for them, than even for us. (2012, 7–8)

We should not expect a specific outcome from being present. Although we can hope that presence can improve a relationship, the focus should be on simply being there without expectations.

Global Context

Eckhart Tolle (2005) believes that there is an awakening occurring on the planet. The first chapter of *The New Earth* is entitled "The Flowering of Human Consciousness," wherein he writes:

> What is arising now is not a new belief system, a new religion, spiritual ide-ology, or mythology. We are coming to the end not only of mythologies but also of ideologies and belief systems. The change goes deeper than the con-tent of your mind, deeper than your thoughts. In fact, at the heart of the new

consciousness lies the transcendence of thought, the newfound ability of rising above thought, of realizing a dimension within yourself that is infinitely more vast than thought. You then no longer derive your identity, your sense of who you are, from the incessant stream of thinking that in the old consciousness you take to yourself. What a liberation to realize that the "voice in my head" is not who I am. Who am I then? The one who sees that. The awareness that is prior to thought, the space in which the thought – or the emotion or sense perception – happens. (22)

Some believe that a crucial point in this awakening occurred with the picture of the earth taken from the moon in 1968. This picture allowed humanity to see the earth not as a collection of nations on a plastic globe but as something whole and beautiful. Many of the cosmonauts and astronauts were deeply affected. Consider what Edgar Mitchell had to say:

Instead of an intellectual search, there was suddenly a very deep gut feeling that something was different. It occurred when looking at Earth and seeing this blue-and-white planet floating there, and knowing it was seeing it set in the background of the very deep black and velvety cosmos, seeing – rather, knowing for sure – that there was purposefulness of flow, of energy, of time, of space in the cosmos – that it was beyond man's rational ability to understand, that suddenly there was a nonrational way of understanding that had been beyond my previous experience.

There seems to be more to the universe than random, chaotic, purposeless movement of a collection of molecular particles.

On the return trip home, gazing through 240,000 miles of space toward the stars and the planet from which I had come, I suddenly experienced the universe as intelligent, loving, harmonious. (Cited in Kelley 1988, 138)

Rusty Schweichart, (Kelly, 1988) when he looked at the earth passing beneath him, saw it as a whole and even felt something was being born through this witnessing. Although we can trace the roots of the environmental movement back to Henry David Thoreau and John Muir, this movement really began to take hold after this image of the earth.

Ervin Laslo (2009) argues that we are experiencing what he calls "worldshift." Laslo, founder and president of the Club of Budapest, writes, "The need for change is penetrating the thinking of ever more people ... Individually and collectively, as conscious humans and as a conscious species, we are waking up" (xxi).

Paul Hawken, in *Blessed Unrest: How the Largest Movement in the World Came into Being and Why No One Saw It Coming* (2007), provides evidence of the awakening that Tolle and Laslo refer to as he focuses more on a social movement that has arisen from the awakening consciousness. Hawken has travelled around the world giving approximately a thousand talks about the environment. People would come up to him and leave their card after these talks. As he did research into the different groups that appeared on the cards, and inquired into other databases, he concluded that there are between one and two million groups working towards "ecological sustainability and social justice" around the world (2). Hawken felt he was witnessing something "organic, if not biologic" in its growth. He believes this "movement without a name" is the "largest social movement in all of humanity" (4). There are two unstated principles at the core of this movement: "first is the Golden Rule; second is the sacredness of all life, whether it be a creature, child, or culture" (186). He cites the work of Karen Armstrong, who has written about the Axial Age and its central theme of compassion. Hawken argues that compassion and love are "at the heart of the movement," but today is different from the Axial Age:

> I suggest that the contemporary movement is unknowingly returning the favor to the Axial Age, and is collectively forming the basis of an awakening. But it is a very different awakening, because it encompasses a refined understanding of biology, ecology, physiology, quantum physics and cosmology. Unlike the massive failing of the Axial Age, it sees the feminine as sacred and holy, and it recognizes the wisdom of indigenous peoples all over the world, from Africa to Nunavut. (185)

Echoing Tolle, Hawken states that this awakening rejects ideologies and "isms." The movement without a name is clearly coming from the bottom up and is rooted in people's hearts (188).

Hawken's reference to Karen Armstrong (2006, 2011, 2012) is a segue into her work on compassion. Like Hawken, she has travelled around the world speaking to various groups about compassion and has written a book about how we can bring compassion into our life. Most important, she has developed the Charter for Compassion (Armstrong 2012), which states:

> The principle of compassion lies at the heart of all religious, ethical and spiritual traditions, calling us always to treat all others as we wish to be

treated ourselves. Compassion impels us to work tirelessly to alleviate the suffering of our fellow creatures, to dethrone ourselves from the centre of our world and put another there, and to honour the inviolable sanctity of every single human being, treating everybody, without exception, with absolute justice, equity and respect.

It is also necessary in both public and private life to refrain consistently and empathically from inflicting pain. To act or speak violently out of spite, chauvinism, or self-interest, to impoverish, exploit or deny basic rights to anybody, and to incite hatred by denigrating others – even our enemies – is a denial of our common humanity. We acknowledge that we have failed to live compassionately and that some have even increased the sum of human misery in the name of religion.

We therefore call upon all men and women ~ to restore compassion to the centre of morality and religion ~ to return to the ancient principle that any interpretation of scripture that breeds violence, hatred or disdain is illegitimate ~ to ensure that youth are given accurate and respectful information about other traditions, religions and cultures ~ to encourage a positive appreciation of cultural and religious diversity ~ to cultivate an informed empathy with the suffering of all human beings – even those regarded as enemies.

We urgently need to make compassion a clear, luminous and dynamic force in our polarized world. Rooted in a principled determination to transcend selfishness, compassion can break down political, dogmatic, ideological and religious boundaries. Born of our deep interdependence, compassion is essential to human relationships and to a fulfilled humanity. It is the path to enlightenment, and indispensable to the creation of a just economy and a peaceful global community.

The Charter for Compassion has been translated into thirty languages and signed by over ninety thousand people. It is another piece of evidence of the awakening to which Tolle and Hawken refer.

Another instance of this awakening is the example of the country of Bhutan whose societal goal is Gross National Happiness (GNH). Bhutan is a small country in the Himalayas between India and China. Rather than emphasizing consumerism and expanding GDP, they have focused on happiness and well-being. Bhutan aspires to be a wisdom-based culture with this broader perspective. GNH includes four pillars and nine domains within the pillars:

1 Sustainable and equitable socio-economic development (living standards, health, and education)

2 Environmental conservation
3 Promotion of culture (psychological well-being, time use, cultural
   resilience and diversity, and community vitality)
4 Enhancement of good governance (which includes caring for the people,
   accountability, transparency, and other attributes).

The pillars and domains have been broken down into seventy-two vari-
ables (or indicators) that provide means to assess how the country is
meeting its goal of GNH.

In December 2009, along with twenty-three educators with expertise
in holistic and ecological education, I was invited to work with Bhutanese
officials to orient the education system to support the goal of GNH. One
of the outcomes of the workshop was a statement called "Educating
for GNH":

The principles and values of Gross National Happiness are deeply embedded in the consciousness of Bhutanese youth and citizens. They will see
clearly the interconnected nature of reality and understand the full benefits
and costs of their actions. They will not be trapped by the lure of materialism, and will care deeply for others and for the natural world.

HOW: Bhutan's entire educational system will effectively cultivate GNH
principles and values, including deep critical and creative thinking, ecological literacy, practice of the country's profound, ancient wisdom and culture,
contemplative learning, a holistic understanding of the world, genuine care
for nature and for others, competency to deal effectively with the modern
world, preparation for right livelihood, and informed civic engagement.

At the end of the workshop the prime minister was interviewed by one
of the observers, Silver Donald Cameron (2009), who writes for the
Chronicle Herald in Halifax, Nova Scotia. The prime minister of Bhutan,
Lyonchhen Jigmi Y. Thinley, stated:

I would like to see an educational system quite different from the conven-
tional factory, where children are just turned out to become economic animals, thinking only for themselves. I would like to see graduates that are
more *human* beings, with human values, that give importance to relationships, that are eco-literate, contemplative, analytical. I would like graduates
who know that success in life is a state of being when you can come home
at the end of the day satisfied with what you have done, realizing that you
are a happy individual not only because you have found happiness for

yourself, but because you have given happiness, in this one day's work, to your spouse, to your family, to your neighbours – and to the world at large.
http://silverdonaldcameron.com/columns/?m=200912

This holistic vision is very different from most countries in the world that focus on developing workers who can compete in the global economy.

A month after the workshop, principals from all the schools were brought together to begin the process of working towards the vision developed in the workshop and articulated by the prime minister. At beginning of that meeting, Prime Minister Thinley (2010) addressed the principals and identified several areas of focus. He referred to the research on mindfulness meditation and recommended that each day teachers and students engage in meditation for a few minutes. He connected this suggestion to the wisdom traditions in Bhutanese culture:

> And likewise, just a few minutes of contemplation and meditation at the beginning and end of a school day or of a ceremony, ritual, class, assembly, or even sports event can change and deepen the atmosphere on the spot, and bring instant connection with the inner joy that is the essence of GNH ... We are learning personally how to connect directly with these ancient teachings and wisdom that are such a precious part of our heritage. (10)

Schools in Bhutan are called on to be Green Schools with the following dimensions:

- *Environmental Greenery* – Creating the ambience for enriching the experience of living and learning
- *Intellectual Greenery* – Cultivating the gifts of the mind
- *Academic Greenery* – Discovering the grace of great ideas
- *Social Greenery* – Learning to live and learn together
- *Cultural Greenery* – Proclaiming our sense of self and identity
- *Spiritual Greenery* – Looking into ourselves and connecting to a higher level of consciousness
- *Aesthetic Greenery* – Appreciating the beautiful, the graceful, and the tasteful
- *Moral Greenery* – Fostering goodness over cleverness, cooperation over competition, and fair play over victory at any cost.

Bhutan is the first country in the world to make a holistic/ecological vision as a primary focus for their education system.

On 2 April 2012, a one-day meeting was held at the United Nations in New York, convened by Bhutan and entitled "Happiness and Well-Being: Defining a New Economic Paradigm." There were eight hundred people in attendance, including the UN secretary-general, the president of Costa Rica, the presidents of the UN General Assembly and the UN's Economic and Social Council, and representatives from many countries and other individuals spoke in support of the new paradigm. More details about the meeting and the complete statement can be accessed at www.2apr.gov.bt. Policy recommendations based on the new paradigm were sent to all members of the United Nations to consider adopting it in whole or in part.

Other countries, such as the United Kingdom, have also been exploring ways to use Gross National Happiness as a measure of their society's health. The fact that a country with a population of 700,000 has developed a vision that is being considered as an alternative to the consumerist culture is inspiring.

Although one does not have to believe in a global awakening to practise contemplation, the contemplative practitioner may be seen as part of Tolle's "flowering of human consciousness" and Hawken's movement without a name. From this perspective, our individual practice can be seen as part of a process that is potentially healing to the planet and its inhabitants.

Chapter Two

Reflection and Contemplation

Donald Schon's *The Reflective Practitioner: How Professionals Think in Action* (1983) has facilitated much-needed discourse about how individuals working in different professions can reflect on their own practice. Schon argues that the best professional practice is based on reflection. This concept of the reflective practitioner has encouraged people in the professions to view their work as more than mastery of content and technical competence (McKinley and Ross 2007; Bolton 2010). Although Schon's work is extremely valuable, I believe that there is yet another level beyond the reflective practitioner where the person can "live" her or his practice, and this is the contemplative practitioner.

Schon asserts that the professions have tended towards Technical Rationality. At this level, for example, education is simply the recall of knowledge and mastery of technique. According to Schon, Technical Rationality is rooted in positivism, which rests on the premise that empirical science provides the best model for all inquiry and practice. Thus, empiricism has been used as the model not only for the sciences, but also the social sciences and even areas such as philosophy. One of the principal thrusts of twentieth-century philosophy has been analytic philosophy, which rests on positivistic assumptions and abandons metaphysics as nonsensical.

Technical Rationality involves instrumental problem solving and "depends on agreement about ends" (Schon 1983, 41). To solve problems, the person immersed in Technical Rationality usually relies on a model that often is not directly related to practice. Schein (1973) argues that there are three components for professional knowledge based on a positivistic framework that is hierarchical in nature. The basic science component is deemed to be the most important. The three components are:

1 An underlying discipline or basic science component upon which practice rests or from which it is developed.

2 An applied science or "engineering" component from which many of the day-to-day diagnostic procedures and problem-solving solutions are derived.

3 A skills and attitudinal component that concerns the actual performance of services to the client, using the underlying basic and applied knowledge. (43)

From the Technical Rationality perspective, the professions are viewed as applied sciences that are deemed to have less status than the pure sciences. For example, Ernest Greenwood (1966) argues that the scientific method is needed to bolster social work as a profession: "To generate valid theory that will provide a solid base for professional techniques requires the application of the scientific method to the service-related problems of the profession. Continued employment of the scientific method is nurtured by and in turn reinforces the element of rationality" (11).

From the Technical Rationality perspective, the professions are based on science from which the professional learns the more practical skills. These skills are viewed as having lesser status than the knowledge based on the scientific method.

Schon (1983) argues that Technical Rationality has not worked because abstract theory does not inform practice. Practitioners are confronted with problematic situations that are characterized by uncertainty, disorder, and indeterminacy. They can become uncomfortable when they can't account for what they do according to theory. An effective practitioner, instead, operates more intuitively and makes changes based on moment-to-moment decisions. As Richard Bernstein (1976) has submitted, the view of science from a Technical Rationality perspective is inadequate, even at the theoretical level:

There is not a single major thesis advanced by either nineteenth-century Positivists or the Vienna Circle that has not been devastatingly criticized when measured by the Positivists' own standards for philosophical argument. The original formulations of the analytic-synthetic dichotomy and the verifiability criterion of meaning have been abandoned. It has been effectively shown that Positivists' understanding of the natural sciences and the formal disciplines is grossly oversimplified. (207)

Following Schon's argument, the technical approach to teaching has not been effective either. Teachers constantly find themselves in new situations without precedent. Jean Erdman (1987) suggests that teaching, by its very nature, pushes educators into areas of ambiguity and uncertainty. From this perspective, the technical approach to teaching is simply inadequate because it is not flexible enough.

Reflection-in-Action

As an alternative to Technical Rationality, Schon (1983) presents his view of reflection as a more artistic, intuitive process. Embedded in his conception of reflection is Michael Polanyi's (1962) tacit knowing that involves an intuitive sense of how to do things that cannot always be explained in explicitly conceptual terms. Polyani states, "The aim of a skillful performance is achieved by the observance of a set of rules which are not known as such to the person following them" (49). Reflection-in-action, then, refers to a skilful performance and tends to have the following qualities:

- There are actions, recognitions, and judgments which we know how to carry out spontaneously; we do not have to think about them prior to or during their performance.
- We are often unaware of having learned to do these things; we simply find ourselves doing them.
- In some cases, we were once aware of the understandings which were subsequently internalized in our feeling for the stuff of action. In other cases, we may never have been aware of them. In both cases, however, we are usually unable to describe the knowing which our action reveals. (54)

Schon (1983) cites examples from baseball and music to explain his point. For example, the pitcher in baseball is constantly making adjustments to keep ahead of the hitters. He will change speeds and move the ball to different locations, and this process, again, tends to be intuitive rather than rational. In jazz, the players will improvise in a spontaneous way as they collectively develop a feel for the music and what combination of notes is appropriate at different moments. In teaching, the teacher will shift gears in the lesson plan to reach the student in that particular situation if he or she comes to a "teachable moment" based on an intuition of what is right.

Reflection-in-action can focus on a variety of elements. The practitioner, for example, may deal with the tacit norms underlying a particular decision, or on the appropriate strategy that is implicit in his or her behaviour. Alternatively, the practitioner may reflect on the right feeling that can develop in approaching a problem, the way she has framed a problem, or on the appropriate role that she can play in solving the problem. In short, reflection-in-action weaves together practice and theory at an intuitive level.

The reflective practitioner may reframe the problem several times as the setting of the problem is probably more important than the problem-solving procedures themselves. For example, Schon (1983) states that 80 to 85 per cent of cases faced by an ophthalmologist do not fall into the "book" of standard diagnoses. The doctor must constantly look for new ways to diagnose and treat cases that come to her. Likewise, the teacher is always being confronted with new situations that require new solutions.

Schon (1983) quotes Lev Tolstoy to give an example of reflection-in-action in education:

> Every individual must, in order to acquire the art of reading in the shortest possible time, be taught quite apart from any other and therefore there must be a separate method for each. That which forms an insuperable difficulty to one does not in the least keep back another, and vice versa. One pupil has a good memory and it is easier for him to memorize the syllables than to comprehend the vowellessness of the consonants; another reflects calmly and will comprehend a most rational sound method; another has a fine instinct, and he grasps the law of word combinations by reading whole words at a time.
>
> The best teacher will be he who has at his tongue's end the explanation of what it is that is bothering the pupil. These explanations give the teacher the knowledge of the greatest possible number of methods, the ability of inventing new methods and, above all, not a blind adherence to one method but the conviction that all methods are one-sided, and that the best method would be the one which would answer best to all the possible difficulties incurred by a pupil, that is, not a method but an art and talent.
>
> Every teacher must ... by regarding every imperfection in the pupil's comprehension, not as a defect of the pupil, but as a defect of his own instruction, endeavor to develop in himself the ability of discovering new methods. (65–6)

In a sense, the teacher is an on-the-spot researcher who must be ready with new methods based on an intuitive sense of what is appropriate for the student that she is dealing with. As a result of this notion, researchers at the Massachusetts Institute of Technology have undertaken a program of in-service education for teachers, based on the idea of reflection-in-action (Schon 1983, 66). Educators (e.g., Minott 2010; Reagan, Case, and Brubacher 2000) have advocated teacher reform based on the concept of the reflective practitioner.

Presence and Contemplation

But is reflection enough? I would argue that there is an element that is necessary to good practice that is not included in the notion of reflection. This is the quality of Presence, which was discussed in chapter 1. Perhaps the best example of Presence comes from music, as it is not enough for a pianist just to be a good technician or even to play the music with the right intuitive sense. In listening to music, we look for more than technique and musicianship; we also seek to be moved, and it is the musician's depth of character – or Presence – that raises the performance to that level. Certainly, what draws us to a Horowitz or Ashkenazy performance is not just the technical proficiency, but the depth and warmth of the performance.

Good teachers also evoke this quality of depth, which Emerson (2003) so aptly captures in a talk he gave to teachers:

> According to the depth from which you draw your life, such is the depth not only of your strenuous effort, but of your manners and presence. The beautiful nature of the world has here blended your happiness with your power … Consent yourself to be an organ of your highest thought, and lo! suddenly you put all men in your debt, and are the fountain of an energy that goes pulsing on with waves of benefit to the borders of society, to the circumference of things. (484)

Clearly, we are talking about another level of experience that is beyond sense experience and even reflection. At this level, then, we also connect with a larger reality (e.g., the Tao, Jung's collective unconscious, Bohm's implicate order) that is much different from the empiricist's notion of an objective reality, or the conception of personal knowledge based on individual construction of meaning requiring commitment and reflection. This level, the *contemplative practitioner*, is realized through various forms of contemplation.

Drawing on the thought of St. Bonaventure, a favourite philosopher of Western mystics, Ken Wilber (1983) cites three levels of experience that correspond to the levels discussed here: Technical Rationality, Reflection, and Presence. St. Bonaventure describes three modes of knowing or three "eyes." The first eye is of the flesh where we perceive the external world of space, time, and objects. The second eye is reason where we know through philosophy, logic, and reflection. The third eye is that of contemplation where we gain knowledge of transcendent realities. At this level, the distinction between subject and object disappears. Wilber notes:

> Further said St. Bonaventure, all knowledge is a type of illumination. There is exterior and inferior illumination (*lumen exterius* and *lumen inferius*), which lights the eye of flesh and gives us knowledge of sense objects. There is *lumen interius*, which lights the eye of reason and give us knowledge of philosophical truths. And there is *lumen superius*, the light of transcendent Being which illumines the eye of contemplation and reveals salutary truth, "truth which is unto liberation." (3)

Wilber (1983) also submits that St. Bonaventure's three levels correspond with those of Hugh of St. Victor (first of the great Victorine mystics) who distinguished between *cogitatio*, *meditatio*, and *contemplatio*. *Cogitatio* is empiricism and thus is based on knowing of the facts of the external world. *Meditatio* involves internal reflection and seeking the truths of the mind. *Contemplatio*, again, is beyond duality "whereby the psyche or soul is united instantly with Godhead in transcendent insight (revealed by the eye of contemplation)" (4).

Although Wilber (1983) has cited Christian mystics, these three eyes can be found in other mystical and philosophical traditions. For example, the Hindus speak of a third eye, which is the eye of Presence. Immanuel Kant spoke of three levels of knowing, which correspond roughly to the levels cited above, and include (1) sensibility – sense experience, (2) understanding – conceptual and scientific intelligence, and (3) reason which intuits transcendent ideas.

Wilber (1983) claims that the three levels are nested and that each of the three levels cited by St. Bonaventure and Hugh of St. Victor transcends the previous level. Thus, the eye of the mind includes and transcends the eye of the flesh. The eye of the mind includes sense experience but also contains ideas, images, concepts, and logic. At this level, we can reflect on our sense experience and use images and concepts to facilitate the reflection. Also, we can confine ourselves to the level of the mind in an area such as mathematics. However, it is an error to reduce the level of reason to the level of flesh. This kind of reductionism ignores the unique features of each level. Thus, contemplation transcends, yet includes, the previous two levels.

Consider the relationship between practice and theory. From the Technical Rationality viewpoint, theory is seen as separate from and superior to practice. Yet, people working in the professions are often confused by a problematic situation where what they do does not fit the theory. Reflection-in-action answers this dilemma. Practice and theory are interwoven in a dialectical process of framing the problem and on-the-spot experimenting in a reflective conversation with the unique situation at hand. From the perspective of Presence, there is a synthesis of theory/practice and duality disappears. Theory and practice are experienced as a unity.

Presence has been called the Self (Jung), the Atman (Hinduism), our Buddha-nature (Buddhism), or the Soul (Moore 1992). Thomas Merton (1959), an American Trappist monk, speaks of the "inner self," which is another description of Presence:

> Instead of seeing the external world in its bewildering complexity, separateness, and multiplicity; instead of seeing objects as things to be manipulated for pleasure or profit; instead of placing ourselves over against objects in a posture of desire, defiance, suspicion, greed or fear, the inner self sees the world from a deeper and more spiritual viewpoint. In the language of Zen, it (the inner self) sees things "without affirmation or denial"; that is to say, from a higher vantage point, which is intuitive and concrete and which has no need to manipulate or distort reality by means of slanted concepts and judgments. It simply "sees" what it sees and does not take refuge behind a screen of conceptual prejudices and verbalistic distortions. (17)

Merton (1959) speaks of intuition as an aspect of Presence, but is this the same as the intuition of Schon (1983) Francis Vaughn (1979) speaks of levels of intuition, and three of her levels can be linked with Wilber's (1983) different eyes. The first level of intuition is what Vaughn calls the "physical level" where the body or the flesh reacts instinctively to a situation. For example, muscle tension can indicate stress in a person's life.

The next level is the mental, which parallels the eye of reason. At the mental level, intuition is sometimes expressed through images, just as we may have flashes of insight that can lead to inquiry. This level is similar to Schon's (1983) reflective practitioner level where the individual uses moment-to-moment insight to help in the problem-solving process.

The highest level of intuition in Vaughn's (1979) framework is the spiritual, which parallels the eye of contemplation. Here intuition is independent from feelings, thoughts, and sensations. Vaughn comments, "Paradoxically, the cues on which intuition depends on the other levels are regarded as interference at this level" (77). At this level, intuition moves beyond dualism to experience unity directly. The following statement by Teilhard de Chardin (1965) is an example of spiritual intuition:

The farther and more deeply we penetrate into matter, by means of increasingly powerful methods, the more we are confounded by the interdependence of its parts. Each element of the cosmos is positively woven from all the others ... It is impossible to cut into this network, to isolate a portion without it becoming frayed and unravelled at all its edges. All around us, as far as the eye can see, the universe holds together, and only one way of considering it is really possible, that is, to take it as a whole, in one piece. (43–4)

Phenomenologically, Presence is experienced as unmediated awareness. This awareness is characterized by openness, by a sense of relatedness, and by awe and wonder. When we experience Presence, duality drops away, and as teachers, we see part of ourselves in our students. At the deepest level, we may experience brief moments of communion with our students. For example, Samuel Freedman (1990) describes how one teacher, Jessica Siegel, has each of her high school students write an autobiography, and through this process she develops a communal bond with each student:

Every year she finishes the autobiographies feeling the same way. Her students are heroes ... How they fill her with awe. How they, yes, inspire her ... When she reads their words, when she hears their voices, when she can practically grasp their urgent breath in this empty room, she knows her life has a reason. (68–9)

Teachers frequently can speak of how their students can instil in them a sense of wonder. For example, Marcia Umland (cited in Macrorie 1984), an elementary school teacher, states, "I get exhausted, but not burned out. Sometimes I'm dropping my dream for a day or two, but most days I'm on, and stunned by the kids" (161). At this level, we can see our students as Zen masters who with their directness can awaken us if we remain open. We need to keep the kind of openness suggested by Emerson (2003):

If a child happens to show that he knows any fact about astronomy, or planets, or birds, or rocks, or history that interests him and you, hush all the classes and encourage him to tell it so that all may hear. Then you have made your school-room like the world. Of course you will insist on modesty in the children and respect to their teachers, but if the boy stops you in your speech, cries out that you are wrong and sets you right, hug him! (484)

The Contemplative Practitioner

Margret Buchmann (1989) claims that contemplation includes "careful attention and quiet wonder" (39). The wonder can arise from the unmediated experience of contemplation. Contemplation can occur spontaneously, or the person can engage in contemplative practices such as meditation. Here are some examples of spontaneous forms of contemplation:

> A traveler leaning against a tree listens to the sounds of the breeze rustling the treetops and barely senses his own breath; it is as though he had "become" the wind.

> An elderly Jew, draped in his impressively trimmed prayer shawl and black cubes of leather (*tefillin*) sways back and forth in the dawn light, monotonously repeating a simple prayer which brings him exaltation.

> A vacationer lies on the beach, giving herself over quietly to the sun and the air, engulfed by the lulling rhythms of the sea.

> A man hears organ tones cascading through a cathedral; as they vibrate through him, he is carried into a reverie where memories and images of childhood flood him – he has become a child again.

> A camper gazes into a lowering fire following the trail of the flowing ashes as they drift upward and fade into darkness; she feels as though she, too, were floating gently through space.

> A rock climber on a mountaintop breathes in the silence above the earth; he is shaken by its immensity and his mind becomes as still as the snows in the mountain passes. (Carrington 1977, 3–4)

Meditation

While the above experiences are examples of spontaneous contemplation, there have been various disciplines that are designed to enhance contemplation. These practices include meditation and various types of body work such as Qigong, yoga, aikido, archery, and tai chi. I have been involved in introducing meditation practice to teachers for the past twenty-five years and this work is described in chapter 7.

The task of meditation focuses on being aware of what is happening in the present moment. By quieting down, we begin to watch and let go of the ego-chatter in our heads. It is the ego-chatter that forms the main barrier to Presence and can seem to run on endlessly. Meditation practice allows us to see how our thoughts can often control our behaviour. For example, during meditation, the thought can arise that I need to buy that new jacket, and instead of simply reacting to the thought I watch the thought arise and disappear in my consciousness. Through meditation, we learn that we can witness our thoughts rather than merely run on "automatic pilot" where we simply react unconsciously to our thoughts. In other words, *we don't have to believe what we think*.

The goal of meditation is to rest in that place that Merton (1959) referred to beyond thought and concept – a place of direct awareness. In the meditation process, the focus is not on analysing or reflecting on the thoughts, but moving to a place of spacious awareness. In this place of direct awareness, we can feel a deep connectedness to the world around us.

Taisen Deshimaru (1985), a Zen master, says, "Once the ego has disappeared there is no more duality. As soon as there is myself and others, that is duality. When there is no more me there are no more others; there is interdependence" (19).

Conclusion

Until very recently, the contemplative element has been ignored in education and Western society generally. As discussed in chapter 1, there is evidence that contemplation and contemplative practices are becoming more prominent. In the past fifteen years, we have seen the establishment of institutions like the Center for Contemplative Mind in Society (www. contemplativemind.org) and the Garrison Institute (www.garrisoninstitute. org). Both of these institutions have done important work in bringing contemplative practices into a variety of settings. They have also conducted important research on contemplative practices, which is discussed in chapter 6.

We need both reflection and contemplation; the two processes complement each other. Contemplation opens us to direct, unmediated experience, while reflection allows for analysis and understanding experience. The contemplative practitioner engages in both reflection and contemplation and moves from one to the other where appropriate. The line between reflection-in-action and contemplation is a fine one. One of the distinguishing factors identified by Buchmann's definition is that contemplation can lead to "wonder" and awe. Michael Lerner (2000) has stated that awe and wonder should be the first goals of education. If so, then contemplation and contemplative practices have an important role in teaching and learning.

Chapter Three

Contemplative Practices

In the West, we have tended to associate meditation with gurus and mysticism. This is unfortunate. Meditation is a simple practice that focuses on the development of attention. Through meditation practice, we develop our ability to attend to what is happening throughout the day. Gradually, we begin to notice that we can focus more easily. One of my students who was studying for her comprehensive examination ("comps") put it this way: "My ability to concentrate on my work after meditating seems greater. Getting closer to 'comps' and such, my ability to retain what I'm reading I feared was diminishing. But today I noticed an alertness, an attention to my work, which I began after meditating." The attention we develop through meditation not only can help in our work, but also can enrich the little moments during the day. We seem to become more aware of the beauty in nature, the joy of children at play, and yes, more attuned to the suffering of others. Attention connects us more deeply with everything that is happening around us.

As indicated in chapter 1, there are many physiological and psychological benefits to meditation (Smalley and Winston 2010, xvii). Some of the benefits include lowered heart rate, reduced blood pressure, heightened perception, increased empathy, reduced anxiety, relief from addiction, alleviation of pain, and improvements in memory and learning ability. Meditation has also been linked to the reversal of heart disease. Along with other changes, such as improvements in diet and exercise, Dean Ornish (1990) has found that meditation is an important factor in reversing heart illness.

In related research, Redford Williams (1989) suggests that lifestyle changes such as meditation are important to the development of the "trusting heart." Williams finds that what is particularly damaging to the heart is hostility and anger. People who carry hostility are more prone to heart attack than the average population. In contrast, people who have trusting hearts have a much greater chance to be healthy:

> The trusting heart believes in the basic goodness of humankind, that most people will be fair and kind in relationships with others. Having such beliefs, that trusting heart is slow to anger. Not seeking out evil in others, not expecting the worst of them, the trusting heart expects mainly good from others and, more often than not, finds it. As a result, the trusting heart spends little time feeling resentful, irritable, and angry.
>
> From this it follows that the trusting heart treats others well, with consideration and kindness; the trusting heart almost never wishes or visits harm upon others. Just as our research has shown that the hostile heart is at risk of premature death and disease, it also can reassure us that the trusting heart appears protected against these outcomes. (71)

To develop the trusting heart, Williams offers a twelve-point program. Some of the recommendations are meditative in nature, as he suggests:

- Monitor your cynical thoughts.
- Practise the relaxation response.
- Force yourself to listen more. (195–6)

Monitoring your thoughts is a form of meditation where we mindfully watch the thoughts as they arise. Meditation allows the individual to be less caught up in his or her thoughts through the process of compassionate awareness. The relaxation response is actually a form of meditation recommended by Herbert Benson (1976) where the individual focuses his or her attention on repeating the number "one." Finally, listening more is another form of meditation. Meditation can actually be described as "deep listening" where we attune ourselves to what is happening within and outside ourselves.

Meditation allows us to feel more comfortable with ourselves and "at home" with the world around us. One of my students makes this point:

> Now when I have difficulty at the beginning of the meditation, sometimes even into ten minutes or so, I just keep with it. I can now "work through" the initial difficulty of blocking out noises and tension. I now know what the benefits are if one perseveres. There is also a wonderful feeling of getting

beyond the busyness and of feeling detached from the nonsense. It's giving me a new way for viewing my daily activities.

There has been a great deal of research on meditation since the first edition of this book was published in 1994. One of the leading researchers has been Richard Davidson (2012), who has conducted a variety of studies on the impact of meditation on the brain and on attention. He has found that meditation is very helpful in reducing the chatter in our minds and helps us focus more clearly (211). Some of his other findings include:

- Compassion meditation strengthens connections between the prefrontal cortex and other brain regions important for empathy.
- Compassion meditation also likely facilitates Social Intuition. (224)

Compassion meditation is where the person focuses on the well-being of others. Social Intuition refers to our ability to read the cues that others give us about their emotional and mental state. Meditation seems to help people become more aware through reading people's body language and non-verbal behaviour. More research on meditation is reviewed in chapter 6.

Meditation is not a cure-all. However, we do have enough evidence to suggest that it is useful in countering stress and in increasing our efficiency in day-to-day living. Another reason for practising meditation relates to the stages of adult development. Carl Jung suggests that, after thirty-five, an individual's basic concerns are of an inward nature. As the finiteness of life becomes more apparent, there is a tendency to be less concerned with the opinions of others and there is more focus on the inner life (LeShan 1974, 172). Another way of putting this is that spiritual concerns become paramount after the age of thirty-five. Jung also stated that most psychological difficulties after age thirty-five stem from spiritual concerns and that once these concerns were dealt with the psychological problems were usually resolved. Meditation can be useful to the individual in dealing with this shift in concerns and can be an important key to adult growth and integration.

A Meditative Stance

This chapter outlines several meditative techniques; however, before describing these, it can be helpful to discuss attitudes that help support meditative practice.

Openness

Each meditation is a new experience. If we approach each sitting as a fresh experience without preconceived expectations, we have already made significant progress in our meditation practice. If we can come to each sitting with an open mind, we are already on the meditative path. However, if we come with a specific set of expectations for each sitting, we already have a model in our head of what should happen. For example, if yesterday's meditation was peaceful, but I find today's meditation is filled with troubling thoughts, I need to let go of yesterday's experience. If I judge today's experience in relation to yesterday's meditation, I will make today's practice even more problematic than it actually is. Meditation involves releasing models and expectations.

Release

Release, or letting go, is fundamental to our practice. Our mind tends to cling to pleasure and to push away unpleasant thoughts. This clinging and pushing away is so fundamental to our thinking that we are hardly even aware of it. Yet, if we watch this grasping and pushing away, we realize how fatiguing it actually is. Why not simply let go of our attempts to cling to what we feel is pleasant? At a deeper level, we can become aware that at some level everything is changing and impermanent and our attempts to grasp and hold on are futile. If we approach meditation with an attitude of letting go, our meditation practice and, indeed, our life becomes much lighter. The heaviness comes from our grasping. We grasp for so much – material goods, pleasure, and to control other people. To see meditation as a process of release is a major step on the meditative path.

Being, Not Doing

We tend to be task oriented in our lives. If we are not working, we can feel we must fill our lives with other activities so that we have "accomplished" something. Even in our leisure hours, we can feel hounded by the pressure to produce. Meditation requires a different stance. It is not a task to be performed. Instead, we practise doing nothing. This is so hard for most of us. When I first tell my students that they will be doing some form of meditation in my class as a requirement, they can often become upset. Their reaction often can be: "How can you do this to me, I am a busy person; I don't have the time to just sit and do nothing." Gradually, however, most of my students end up looking forward to the meditation time as they find it nourishing. One of the reasons it is so nourishing is that we are not performing. We simply are. We begin to accept ourselves without judgment.

Acceptance

In meditation, we gradually learn to accept all that happens. We don't push things away. Many thoughts, images, and feelings can arise during meditation, and our first instinct is to push some of them away. For example, one of my students had worked with a friend who died of AIDS, and during her meditation images and memories of these events came up. At first, she was upset as many of the thoughts and memories were painful. However, after a while, she realized the meditation was allowing her to accept the experience at a deeper level. Sometimes, if we are repressing something that has happened, meditation will allow us to work with it and integrate the experience. This acceptance can lead to a sense of wholeness.

Big Mind, Long Enduring Mind

There are certain metaphors regarding the mind that are helpful in approaching meditation practice. One metaphor is to see our minds as large, like the sky. If our minds are large, irritating thoughts and feelings are seen as rather insignificant. Thoughts become like clouds that float by. When I am flying in an airplane, I love to look out and see the clear blue sky that stretches almost forever. It reminds me of the big mind. In contrast, if we see our minds as small and restricted, our thoughts have little room, and as a result, we can't let go of them. The thoughts take over.

Also helpful is the notion of the long, enduring mind. The long, enduring mind is the patient mind that can wait and deal with all that arises. The long, enduring mind knows that what arises, eventually passes away. In our culture, we tend to focus on the short term whether it be profits or test results. It would be wiser to take the longer view. With the longer view, we watch things from a bigger perspective, and thus, we do not "react" all the time. This does not mean we are not present, it just means we are not constantly weighing and reacting to everything that happens to us. When we are constantly reacting, we become agitated and tired. The long, enduring mind is a mind at peace.

Grace

Grace is not often a term associated with meditation practice particularly when we use a meditation approach based on Eastern spiritual practice. However, I believe it is helpful to see meditation as a grace, or gift. We must have a certain level of privilege and leisure to do meditation. People who are struggling to survive day to day usually cannot meditate. In this sense, we can see meditation as a gift since we have been presented with circumstances in our life so that we can do the practice. Approaching meditation with an attitude of grace means that we are thankful for this opportunity.

The other aspect of grace is that, at some level, we can acknowledge that meditation allows us to be connected to something larger than ourselves. Whether we call this something more God, Christ, Krishna, or Buddha is not the issue. Meditation can let us feel a part of something that, although unseen, is quite wonderful. This is the invisible world described in chapter 5, and that realm can be nourishing and sustaining. To be in contact with this world, even for a moment, is an act of grace.

When we meditate, it is not so important that we keep all of these points in mind. To be rather mundane, the important thing is to "just do it." If we simply approach meditation with an openness, everything takes care of itself; a process unfolds. We don't have to believe in anything, we just need to watch. Of course, teachings can be helpful in the process. To approach meditation, or any spiritual practice, we don't abandon a natural scepticism. I know about natural scepticism since I come from the "show me" state, Missouri. Natural scepticism is not cynicism but simply testing what we hear or read against our experience and common sense. We need to avoid embracing meditation or any spiritual practice as *the* answer. Meditation is a method or practice; it helps us along our journey, but there is much more to the journey than meditation.

Forms of Meditation

When one is just beginning meditation practice, it is helpful to pick a method you feel comfortable with. It is possible to categorize approaches to meditation according to four different types: intellectual, emotional, physical, and action-service.

Intellectual/Inquiry

These approaches to meditation focus on awareness and discrimination. Meditation is seen as a form of inquiry into the mind-body process. This is not inquiry as we traditionally use in the West, which is viewed as problem solving; instead, meditation is an investigation into the basic processes of life. Insight, or *vipassana* meditation, can be looked at in this light. Krishnamurti also practised a form of meditative inquiry. He would take a question and then explore it completely. For example, Krishnamurti (1963) was asked, How is one to be intelligent? His reply was:

> What is implied in this question? You want a method by which to be intelligent – which implies that you know what intelligence is. When you want to go some place, you already know your destination and you only have to ask the way. Similarly, you think you know what intelligence is, and you want a method by which you can be intelligent. Intelligence is the very questioning of the method. Fear destroys intelligence, does it not? Fear prevents you from examining, questioning, inquiring; it prevents you from finding out what is true. Probably you will be intelligent when there is no fear. So you have to inquire into the whole question of fear, and be free of fear; and then there is the possibility of you being intelligent. But if you say, "How am I to be intelligent?" you are merely cultivating a method and so you become stupid. (40)

Emotional

These forms of meditation connect with the heart. Mantra meditation, which involves repeating a phrase or word over and over, tends to be emotionally oriented. One of the classic mantras is the Jesus prayer, "Lord Jesus, Son of God, have mercy on me." *The Way of the Pilgrim*, a classic in the spiritual literature, describes how a Russian monk travelling in Russia constantly repeated the Jesus prayer and how this process transformed him and those he met. In the Hindu religion, the devotee recites the name of God, Ram, as a mantra.

Physical

These meditations involve various forms of movement. Hatha yoga, tai chi, aikido, and Qi Gong are movement meditations. The practitioner brings full attention to the physical movement. This type of meditation can appeal to people who find it difficult to sit for long periods and need to move. Lawrence LeShan (1974) describes an example of movement meditation:

> There is the Hasidic tale of the great Rabbi who was coming to visit a small town in Russia. It was a very great event for the Jews in the town and each thought long and hard about what questions they would ask the wise man. When he finally arrived, all were gathered in the largest available room and each was deeply concerned with the questions they had for him. The Rabbi came into the room and felt the great tension in it. For a time, he said nothing and then began to hum softly a Hasidic tune. Presently all there were humming with him. He then began to sing the song and soon all were singing with him. Then he began to dance and soon all present were deeply involved in the dance, all fully committed to it, all just dancing and nothing else. In this way, each one became whole with himself, each healed the splits within himself which kept him from understanding. After the dance went on for a time, the Rabbi gradually slowed it to a stop, looked at the group, and said, "I trust that I have answered all your questions." (50–1)

Action Meditation

These meditations are service oriented. One works in the world with the idea that each act is done with non-attachment to results. The action is not viewed as a way of improving or changing the world. Instead, the action is performed as an offering to the universe without attachment to a particular outcome. In Hinduism, this is called "karma yoga." In performing acts of service, we can experience connectedness:

> Or in service itself – comforting a crying child, reassuring a frightened patient, bringing a glass of water to a bedridden elder – when you feel yourself to be a vehicle of kindness, an instrument of love. There's more to the deed than the doer and what's been done. You yourself feel transformed and connected to a deeper sense of identity. (Dass and Gorman 1985, 39)

Here our daily life is seen as grist for the mill where our relationships with others, including our family and friends, can offer many challenges and opportunities for being more aware. One of my students, for example, who was the mother of two girls, found that she felt a distance between herself and her older daughter. There were not any major difficulties but there was little physical affection. The mother decided to listen more and talk less with her daughter during the course she was taking with me. Towards the end of the course, she was surprised that her daughter began to snuggle up beside her when they were watching television. She attributed this to simply being more present to her daughter. In the past, she had been quick to offer solutions to problems her daughter was dealing with. She found it difficult in the beginning to keep quiet and listen, but after a while she began to be more comfortable just listening. She was not expecting a particular outcome but was delighted when her daughter became more affectionate. This is a little "miracle of mindfulness."

Meditation Practices

Insight

Insight, or *vipassana* meditation, focuses on being aware of what happens in each moment. This meditation usually starts with an awareness of the flow of the breath. One simply follows either the breath coming in and out of the nostrils or the rising and falling of the abdomen. The eyes are usually closed, and we may label the flow of the breath with "in and out" for the nostrils or "rising and falling" for the abdomen. Insight meditation, however, does not stay with the breath as the sole focus. Although breathing is the anchor to which we can always return, the awareness gradually moves to other phenomena. For example, awareness can focus on the sensations that may arise in the body. If our knee starts to hurt, or our arm itches, our attention can shift to these sensations. The mind simply notices these sensations as they arise and stays focused on them and then notices them passing away. The term *insight* is based, to a large extent, on watching this arising and passing away of phenomena.

Another area that we can focus on is our feelings. For example, if we have had an argument with our spouse, we can be filled with anger. Emotions can sometimes be so very powerful that they can "take over," and we lose our basic awareness of what is happening. Here we can come back to the breathing to gain our balance and then return to an awareness of the anger. Insight can come from witnessing that we are not the anger, which arises and then passes away. Yes, there are these emotions, but because they are impermanent we gain understanding that we don't have to identify with or become them.

Another area of focus is our thoughts. Our mind is filled with thoughts, and sometimes they can be overwhelming. For example, thoughts relating to our work can be quite strong, and during our meditation we simply try to stay aware of these thoughts. One technique for watching our thoughts is to see them as clouds floating by. Another technique is to label the thoughts. At a general level, we can label all thoughts as "thinking," or we can be more specific and label the nature of the thoughts. For example, we can use labels like planning, remembering, or imagining. Shunryu Suzuki Roshi (1970) gives some helpful advice when observing our thoughts. They relate to the metaphor of "big mind" discussed earlier:

> When you are practicing Zazen meditation do not try to stop your thinking. Let it stop by itself. If something comes into your mind, let it come in and let it go out. It will not stay long. When you try to stop your thinking, it means you are bothered by it. Do not be bothered by anything. It appears that the something comes from outside your mind, but actually it is only the waves of your mind and if you are not bothered by the waves, gradually they will become calmer and calmer … If you leave your mind as it is, it will become calm. This mind is called big mind. (34)

Another focus for the insight process is sound. If any sound arises, our attention turns to the sound. If a car passes outside or someone turns on the television in the next apartment, we notice the sound, and then return to the breathing again as our anchor.

Eventually, with insight meditation, our attention shifts to whatever is predominant in the moment. If my back is sore, my attention shifts to the soreness. If my thoughts start to react to the pain, I notice these thoughts. If any related emotions arise, I notice these. If my mind becomes too unsettled by all this, I simply return to the breath. Gradually, however, this meditation allows me to live in the present moment. It allows our natural awareness to arise so that we are not encumbered by our thoughts and emotions. We experience more fully each moment rather than living in the past or projecting ourselves into the future. We gradually learn that all we really have to experience is what is happening right now.

One of the best books on insight meditation is Joseph Goldstein's *The Experience of Insight: A Natural Unfolding* (1976). In this book, Goldstein says:

> Just let things happen as they do. Let all images and thoughts and sensations rise and pass away without being bothered, without reacting, without judging, without clinging, without identifying with them. Become one with the big mind, observing carefully, microscopically, all the waves coming and going. This attitude will quickly bring about a state of balance and calm.

Don't let the mind get out of focus. Keep the mind sharply aware, moment to moment of what is happening, whether the in-out breath sensations, or thoughts. In each instant be focused on the object with a balanced and relaxed mind. (28)

Mindfulness

Mindfulness is insight meditation applied to everyday life and involves bringing awareness to acts that we do each day. *Mindfulness can be seen as meditation in action.* The rush and noise of our world makes it difficult to be fully present. For example, we may try to relax by going for a walk; but we often take our problems with us on the walk. We can take with us a problem at work, say, or our concern over how to pay the Visa bill, and we find at the end of our walk that we are so preoccupied that we haven't truly experienced the walk. We haven't really felt the air on our face, or looked at the trees, or felt the warmth of the sun. Nature can be very healing as we experience it directly, but our thoughts get in the way; our preoccupations and thoughts can be a barrier to the world.

Another example of how it is difficult to be mindful is how we often try to do several things at once. At home, I can be watching television, reading the paper, and trying to carry on a conversation with my wife. In our attempts to fit everything in, our consciousness becomes fragmented. Our presence is diminished.

Another word for mindfulness is wholeheartedness, when we do something we do it completely. Our consciousness is whole. Because mindfulness is so important to reconnecting ourselves with the world around us, I encourage my students to work on being mindful. There are many simple exercises that we can do to be more present. We can start our practice by focusing on doing one thing at a time. For example, the whole experience of preparing a meal, eating, and doing the dishes can be done mindfully. As you cut the celery for the salad, just cut the celery. Don't try to solve the world's problems while you cut the celery. Sometimes, we can be so preoccupied that we can cut ourselves, rather than the celery. Gradually, we find that by just cutting the celery we can do more to heal ourselves and the planet. Being fully present is a profoundly healing act. As we eat the meal, we can focus our attention on the eating, chewing, and swallowing. Often, we read the paper or watch TV while we eat our meals, and as a result, we taste very little. Finally, when doing the dishes, focus on the task. Feel the water as it cascades over your hands and the dishes. Often, we can hardly wait to finish one task so that we can do something else. For example, as I do the dishes, my mind will be on the hockey game, which is about to start on TV. As I watch the hockey game, my mind begins to drift to problems that I may face at work tomorrow. As we do one thing, our mind is on another. We tend to live in the future or the past.

One master of mindfulness is Thich Nhat Hanh, who has written several books on mindfulness. Thich Nhat Hanh (1976, 86–7) suggests a variety of exercises in mindfulness including the following:

CLEANING HOUSE

Divide your work into stages: straightening things and putting away books, scrubbing the toilet, scrubbing the bathroom, sweeping the floors and dusting. Allow a good length of time for each task. Move slowly, three times more slowly than usual. Fully focus your attention on each task. For example, while placing a book on the shelf, look at the book, be aware of what book it is, know that you are in the process of placing it on the shelf, intending to put it in the specific place. Know that your hand reaches for the book, and picks it up. Avoid any abrupt or harsh movement. Maintain mindfulness of the breath, especially when your thoughts wander.

A SLOW-MOTION BATH

Allow yourself thirty to forty-five minutes to take a bath. Don't hurry for even one second. From the moment you prepare the bathwater to the moment you put on clean clothes, let every motion be light and slow. Be attentive of every movement. Place your attention to every part of your body, without discrimination or fear. Be mindful of each stream of water on your body. By the time you've finished, your mind should feel as peaceful and light as your body. Follow your breath. Think of yourself as being in a clean and fragrant lotus pond in the summer.

In another book, Thich Nhat Hanh (1991) suggests a meditation for the telephone:

I recommend that the next time you hear the phone ring, just stay where you are, breathe in and out consciously, smile to yourself, and recite this verse: "Listen, listen. This wonderful sound brings me back to my true self." When the bell rings for the second time, you can repeat the verse, and your smile will be even more solid. When you smile, the muscles of your face relax, and your tension quickly vanishes, you can afford to practice breathing and smiling like this, because if the person calling has something important to say, she will certainly wait for at least three rings. When the phone rings for the third time, you can continue to practice breathing and smiling, as you walk to the phone slowly, with all your sovereignty. You are your own master. (30)

A classic mindfulness exercise is eating a raisin. Usually this involves two raisins. We eat one raisin as we normally would. Next, we eat a raisin mindfully. We can start by looking at the raisin and contemplating it. Through the contemplation, we make friends with the raisin. We are conscious of all the conditions that brought the raisin to us in this moment. These include the earth, rain, and sun that nourished the grape. Then there were people who looked after the grape and harvested it. Others were involved in drying the grape and eventually packaging it and shipping the raisin. People in stores placed its package on the shelves. So many conditions brought the raisin to us. Then we can put the raisin in our mouth and let it sit there for moment. Gradually, we start to chew it slowly, tasting it fully. When we are done, we swallow the remains.

After eating both raisins, I ask students to compare the experience. Invariably students point out the taste of the second raisin was much richer. I have had some students who found this small exercise life changing in that it opened to them the whole world of mindfulness.

I suggest that you start with very simple activities in developing mindfulness. Gradually, you can then bring your attention to more complex situations. Connected to insight sitting practice, mindfulness becomes a powerful way that we can carry our awareness into daily life. With mindfulness, meditation is not something that is fragmented or separated from the rest of life. Instead, our day can become a seamless whole of awareness. We find that we live in the most empowering place, the eternal now.

In chapter 6, I discuss mindfulness in more detail and how it has been incorporated into many aspects of modern life.

Body Scan

The body is an excellent anchor for meditation practice and helps us move away from being just in our heads. Also called body sweeping, this technique has been taught by Jon Kabat-Zinn and S.N. Goenka. Kabat-Zinn (1990) describes his approach in *Full Catastrophe Living: Using the Wisdom of Your Body and Mind to Face Stress, Pain, and Illness*, while Hart details Goenka's wisdom on the body scan in his book, *Vipassana Meditation: As Taught by S.N. Goenka* (1987). The technique starts either at the top of the head or the toes and gradually moves through the entire body. Here are some basic instructions:

> Begin by focusing the attention at the top of the head. Note any sensations there. Do you notice any pulsing, itching, or tightness or is there not any particular sensation that arises? Now move the attention to the back of the head. Again be aware of any sensations there. If there is a sensation, focus on that for the moment. Now shift the attention to the left side of the head and then the right side. What sensations do you notice there? Now focus on the face. Be aware of any sensations that arise around the eyes, nose or mouth.
>
> Now focus on the front of the neck and then gradually move to the sides of the neck and finally the back of the neck. Now gradually move the attention down the back. First, focus on the shoulders and then gradually move to the top of the back. Move slowly down the back noticing any sensation. Tension can be held in the shoulders and the back so move slowly through this area of the body noting any tightness or pain. If there is any pain, try not to react to the pain but just notice it in a non-judgmental manner. Soften the attention where there is pain or tightness.
>
> Shift the awareness now to the arms. Move the attention down the one arm till you reach the hands and the fingers. Again note any sensation or lack thereof. Now move the awareness to the other arm moving the attention down from the shoulder to the hands and fingers.
>
> Focus the attention on the right pelvis area. Now slowly move the awareness down the leg. Focus on the thigh, then the knee. Next scan the lower leg and finally the feet and toes. Shift the attention to the left pelvis area and then move down the leg to the foot and toes noting any sensation that arises. Rest the attention on the feet and toes for a moment.
>
> Now move the awareness back up the body starting with toes and feet and moving through each part again.

After moving through the body slowly, you can follow with body scans that are faster as you sweep up and down. The body scan can take as long forty-five minutes.

Movement Meditations

In movement meditations, we bring heightened awareness to bodily movement. Classic body work includes yoga, tai chi, and Qi Gong. In the first edition of this book, I included drawings of hatha yoga postures, or asanas. Since then there has been an explosion in the practice of yoga in North America, with different forms of yoga being offered in studios and shown on television and DVDs, and I felt there was no need to provide this material in the second edition. As I mention in my story at the end of this book, I have been practising yoga since 1968 and have felt the many benefits of the practice. I believe that some form of body work can also help with sitting meditation. William Broad, in his book *The Science of Yoga: The Risks and the Rewards* (2012), reviews some of the claims regarding yoga. He points out that some postures, such as the headstand, can cause injury and thus hatha yoga should be approached carefully. Based on the research, Broad claims that yoga can heighten powers of concentration, inspire creativity, improve moods, and help cure some physical ailments.

Whatever practice of movement meditation we choose, it is important to bring mindfulness to the movements. It is easy to lose our focus after we have been doing a practice for a time. We can fall into an unconscious routine.

There is the practice of Mindful Yoga where full attention is brought to the movements. Jon Kabat-Zinn (2005) reports how he employs Mindful Yoga in his stress-reduction program. He encourages his patients to start very slowly and practise the postures with gentleness. Gradually, the body loosens up and becomes more flexible. He tells us, "There is nothing quite so wonderful as getting your body down on the floor and working with it gently and systematically and above all, mindfully, using the various asanas and sequences of postures to re-inhabit your body with full awareness and explore lovingly its ever-changing boundaries, limits and capabilities in the present moment" (275). This approach does not have a goal or specific objectives. As Kabat-Zinn submits, there is "only this moment" (276). Mindful Yoga lets us re-inhabit our bodies. Kabat-Zinn believes that our bodies "love the attention" that Mindful Yoga can bring (277).

Walking Meditation

In this practice, there is no destination. We use the lifting, moving, and placing of the foot as our object of attention. Usually, the movement is slow and we only walk about ten or twelve paces and then turn around. We do not need to look down but keep our eyes looking straight ahead. Kabat-Zinn (2005) gives more specific instructions:

> Beginning with lifting just one heel, we then bring awareness to moving that foot and leg forward, and then to the placing of the foot on the ground, usu-

ally first with the heel. As the whole of this now forward foot comes down on the floor or ground, we note the shifting of the weight from the back foot through to the forward foot, and then we note the lifting of the back foot, heel first and later the rest of it as the weight of the body comes fully onto the forward foot, and the cycle continues: moving placing, shifting-lifting, moving placing, shifting. (270)

We can also practise variations on walking meditation. One is to practice what Black Elk suggests, "for the Earth is your Grandmother and Mother and She is sacred. Every step that is taken upon Her should be as a prayer" (cited in Brown 1989, 6). In other words, as we feel our feet touch the ground we can cultivate a sense of reverence for the earth, which is supporting us as we walk.

Mantra

Mantra is simply using a word, or phrase, as a vehicle to awakening. It is repeated over and over in silent sitting meditation or as we do our daily activities. The word, *mantra* "comes from the roots *man*, 'the mind,' and *tri*, 'to cross.' The mantram is that which enables us to cross the sea of the mind" (Easwaran 1977, 43):

> The mantram exists in almost all religions. As mentioned earlier, the Jesus prayer is a Christian mantra. *Hail Mary* used in Catholicism is another Christian mantra. I have already mentioned the mantra, Ram, which Gandhi repeated throughout his life and was on his lips when he died. Other Hindu mantras using Ram include *Om Sri Ram jai Ram jai jai Ram*. This mantra simply means "May Joy prevail." (58)

One of the most famous mantras in Buddhism is *Om mani padme hum* which refers to the "jewel in the lotus of the heart" (60). Here the lotus flower is used as a metaphor for purity of heart which can be realized more fully by repeating this mantra.

In Judaism, the phrase *Barukh, attah Adonai* means "Blessed art thou, O Lord" (Easwaran 1977, 60). By repeating this phrase, the devotee can feel more deeply connected to the divine. In the Muslim faith, the mantra *Bismillah ir-Rahman ir-Rahim* means "In the name of Allah, the merciful, the compassionate" (61). According to Eknath Easwaran, "Orthodox Muslims say this mantram before they speak, as a reminder that everything we say and everything we do should be in accord with the will of God, in accord with the indivisible unity of life" (ibid.).

It is possible to develop your own mantra. One of my students chose the words "thank you" for her mantra. Her name, appropriately, was Grace. Once you have selected a mantra that seems to resonate with you, stick with it. It is wise not to repeat your mantra to individuals who are not sympathetic to meditation practice. The mantra should not necessarily be a secret; it is just that you want to be able to approach meditation practice with a positive frame of mind. Having chosen a mantra, you can begin practice. You can begin with your eyes open and repeat the mantra out loud. Once you have a sense of the sound and the rhythm, you can begin to repeat it silently to yourself with your eyes closed. As you repeat the mantra, get the feeling that the mantra is autonomous, that is, it is repeating itself. You are not doing the mantra, but it is going on within you:

> That is all there is to meditating – just sitting peacefully, hearing the mantra in your mind, allowing it to change any way it wants – to get louder or softer – to disappear or return – to stretch out or speed up ... Meditation is like drifting on a stream in a boat without oars – because you need no oars – you are not going anywhere. (Carrington 1977, 8)

It is possible to repeat your mantra during the day. For example, the mantra can be repeated while riding the bus or subway. At work, if you begin to feel tense, you can work with the mantra to deal with the tension. The mantra can be used when you are walking as it can provide a silent rhythm to your walk. Other opportunities for your mantra include times when you are sick or bored. Occasionally, we are presented with long stretches of time when there is nothing to do. Instead of turning on the TV as relief from our boredom, our mantra can be practised. Another good time for your mantra is when you lie awake at night. Instead of letting random thoughts take over, which can often contribute to restlessness at night, you can repeat the mantra. The silent rhythm can focus the mind and may help you return to sleep.

There are times when it is not appropriate to do your mantra. For example, if you are doing any job or task that requires your full attention, such as driving or listening to music, the mantra will interfere with what you are doing.

Eknath Easwaran (1977) has written a beautiful book on the mantra. In it, he says:

> Once the mantram has become an integral part of our consciousness, all mantrams are the same. Whatever Holy Name we use, at this stage it is the perfect embodiment of the Lord of Love.

The Holy Name reverberating in the depths of consciousness transfigures our entire vision of life. Just as the mantram transforms negative forces in consciousness into constructive power, so it now transforms all our perceptions of the everyday world into unbroken awareness of the unity of life. (246–7)

Visualization

Imagery can be a powerful source of inner growth. An image in our mind can have powerful effects; for example, if I am afraid of public speaking, just the image of seeing myself in front of an audience can make my heart beat faster. Guided imagery, or visualization, attempts to elicit images that can foster positive growth and awareness.

Visualization can bring about specific physiological changes. Studies have shown that when an individual imagines himself or herself running, small contractions take place in the muscles associated with running (Murphy 1992).

We also know that emotional changes can take place through visualization. For example, if we fear flying in an airplane, the image of this event can trigger fear and accompanying physiological changes. Similarly, a relaxing image, such as walking in a meadow, can lead to a lower heart rate, lower blood pressure, and relaxed muscles. Studies have been conducted in a number of areas, and Michael Murphy (1992) claims that these "studies have shown that imagery practice can facilitate relief from various afflictions, among them depression, anxiety, insomnia, obesity, sexual problems, chronic pain, phobias, psychosomatic illnesses, cancer, and other diseases" (372).

A simple visualization exercise to begin with is one in which you visualize an object, such as an orange:

> Set an orange about two or three feet in front of you. Place the orange so that there are no other objects around it to distract your attention ... Relax and breathe deeply ... Now study the orange, notice its shape, color, and any unusual markings, etc. ... Now close your eyes ... See the image of the orange, for example, the shape, color and any markings ... Now open your eyes and look at the orange. Compare it with the image you saw. Notice any differences. Now close your eyes and repeat the exercise.

Another simple and easy exercise is one in which you visualize a room from childhood. This requires recalling a more distant memory image than the orange exercise:

Close your eyes. Imagine yourself in a room you associate with your childhood. Notice the furniture in the room. How is it arranged? Walk to the
window and look out. What do you see? Now look around the room again.
What colors do you notice? Are there any pictures on the wall? What does
the rug look like? Are there any special objects in the room? Finally, notice
the doors. Where do they lead?

Other visualizations can be used to help you gain insight into yourself
and how you deal with various situations:

Close your eyes ... Relax deeply ... You are in a meadow and are feeling
refreshed and invigorated ... You see a path in the meadow and begin to
walk along it. You are enjoying yourself as you take in the scenery, the warmth
of the sun and the fresh air ... You know you are walking in the right direction ... As you continue on the walk you can see an object ahead ... It is getting larger and you can now see that it is a large stone wall ... As you draw
closer to the wall you see that it blocks the path and you cannot get around
the wall or climb over it since it is so high. You now find yourself standing
in front of the wall. What do you do? ... (two minutes) ... Now slowly open
your eyes and reflect on the visualization.

If you have difficulty with this exercise, or with any other, you can come
back to it at another time. You may find that images come easier the next
time. The following guided imagery is more spiritually oriented:

Relax. Close your eyes ... You are in a meadow ... The sky is blue and
you see a hill in the distance ... What does the hill look like as you approach it? ... Is the hill large or small? ... Is it rough and hard to climb or
is its surface smooth and easy to scale? ... You see a path going up the
hill and you follow it ... Is the path wide or narrow? ... What is the ground
like around you as you begin to walk up the path? ... Is there grass or are
there lots of rocks? ... As you walk up this hill notice the view ... Stop and
look around ... How far can you see? ... Now you begin to resume your
walk. Smell the fresh air as you walk up the path. You feel invigorated and
refreshed as you walk up the hill ... .
    You begin to approach the top of the hill and there you see a temple ... As
you approach the temple what does it look like? ... Notice the form of the
building as you approach it. As you approach the temple you feel peaceful
and calm ... You walk to the door of the temple and take your shoes off ...
There is an opening at the top of the temple roof and sunlight is streaming

through ... You walk to the light and stand under it and feel its radiance and warmth ... Let it permeate and rejuvenate your whole being ... You are now ready to go to the inner sanctuary ... There is a symbol or an image in the center of the room ... This symbol represents to you an educational ideal. Reflect on this symbol and its meaning for you ... (Two or three minute pause) ... Leave the temple and walk slowly down the hill ... Now you are reaching the bottom of the hill. Take the energy you have received from this journey and use it as you return to your daily life.

This guided imagery exercise contains a symbol that each person will imagine and interpret in his or her own way. Symbols are integral to the visualization process. Some common symbols found in fantasies and their possible meanings include:

Water: receptivity, passivity, calm
Ascent: growth, inward journey
Cross: tree of life, spiritual connectedness
Hill or mountain: aims or ambitions
Light: creativity, unity, spiritual source
Sun: life force, healing, spiritual wholeness. (Samuels and Samuels 1975, 97)

A symbol can have many meanings, and we should not get too in-volved in interpreting them. However, if a symbol is persistent, you may want to work with it in meditation or other visualizations in order to explore possible meanings.

One of the best books on visualization is *Seeing with the Mind's Eye: The History, Techniques and Uses of Visualization,* by Michael Samuels and Nancy Samuels (1975). This book contains a number of visualizations that can be applied to being more creative, dealing with illness, or simply tapping into our spiritual natures. The following exercise deals with spiritual development:

You are now in a calm, relaxed state of being. To deepen this state you can imagine yourself traveling into space. Visualize yourself drifting weightlessly and effortlessly through space. See the deep blue-black color of space all around you. Watch stars and planets slowly recede as you move past them further and further into space. As you see each star recede, you will become more and more relaxed in a deeper and deeper state of mind. Now visualize an area of diffuse white light ahead of you. Picture yourself moving closer and closer to this area of light until you are bathed by its luminosity and can feel its energy. Travel into the light, toward its center. Visualize the center of the light as a space beyond light and darkness. In this space you will feel open and clear. You will begin to see images before you. Look at them as long as they appear. These are pure images. They have a life of their own, and they will appear and extinguish of their own accord. If any of the images evoke disturbing feelings in you, do not be afraid. Simply allow the images to pass.

Stay in this space as long as you wish. You can receive pure images whenever you go to it. To return to your everyday state of mind simply visualize yourself moving back through space to the place where you started. Count from 1 to 3. Then open your eyes. (156)

If we feel a connection to a particular spiritual teacher, we can visualize the presence of that person. We can imagine the energy, love, and compassion flowing from that person into our own hearts. Visualizing the presence of another person is called *kything*. Louis Savary and Patricia Berne (1988) define kything as a conscious act of spiritual presence. One example of kything that they cite is from Vicktor Frankl's book *Man's Search for Meaning*. One of the ways that Frankl survived in the concentration camp was to imagine the presence of his wife:

As my friend and I stumbled on for miles, slipping on icy spots, supporting each other time and time again, dragging one another up and onward, nothing was said but we both knew; each of us was thinking of his wife. Occasionally I looked at the sky, where the stars were fading and the pink light of the morning was beginning to spread behind a dark bank of clouds. But my mind clung to my wife's image, imagining it with an uncanny acuteness. I heard her answering me, saw her smile, her frank and encouraging look. Real or not, her look was then more luminous than the sun which was beginning to rise. (Cited in Savary and Berne 1988, 68)

In their book, *Kything: The Art of Spiritual Presence* (1988), Savary and Berne talk about three modes of presence – physical, psychological, and spiritual. Kything at the spiritual level can be described as a form of communion.

Loving-Kindness

Sharon Salzberg (1995) is one of the most respected teachers of *metta*, or loving-kindness practice. She writes:

Metta – the sense of love that is not bound to desire, that does not have to pretend that things are other than the way they are – overcomes the illusion of separateness, of not being part of a whole. Thereby metta overcomes all the states that accompany this fundamental error of separateness – fear, alienation, loneliness, and despair – all of the feelings of fragmentation. In place of these, the genuine realization of connectedness brings unification, confidence, and safety. (21)

Metta can be seen in a steady attitude of friendliness: "The culmination of metta is to become a friend to oneself and all of life" (25). Metta is, ultimately, a meditation on how we are connected to people, animals, life, and all creation.

This meditation can either be done as a meditation in itself, or you can combine it with other meditations described above. For example, metta can be done at the beginning or end of a meditation period. Like mantra, metta can also be done during the day while you are standing in line, riding the bus, or doing some other activity that does not demand your total attention. The essence of this meditation is to centre ourselves in the heart area and to contact a basic warmth there. After connecting with the heart, we then attempt to share this warmth and energy with others. There are various forms of loving-kindness, and the one below was taught to me by a Burmese monk, U Silananda. I have made some minor changes in the wording:

May I be well, happy, and peaceful.
May my family be well, happy, and peaceful.
May my friends be well, happy, and peaceful.
May my neighbours be well, happy, and peaceful.
May my colleagues be well, happy, and peaceful.
May all people that I meet be well, happy, and peaceful.
May all people that I am having difficulty with or feel anger towards be well, happy, and peaceful.
May all beings on this planet be well, happy, and peaceful.
May all beings in this universe be well, happy, and peaceful.

This approach starts with those who are emotionally closest to us and then moves out from there. Another approach is to move out geographically:

May I be well, happy, and peaceful.
May all beings in this room be well, happy, and peaceful.
May all beings in this building be well, happy, and peaceful.

May all beings in this neighbourhood be well, happy, and peaceful.
May all beings in this town or city be well, happy, and peaceful.
May all beings in this region be well, happy, and peaceful.
May all beings in this hemisphere be well, happy, and peaceful.
May all beings in this planet be well, happy, and peaceful.
May all beings in this universe be well, happy, and peaceful.

When you are doing the loving-kindness it is also possible to visualize the people that you are sending these thoughts to. I start my classes with this exercise and find that it has added immeasurably to the tone and feel of the class. Many of my students have commented on it as well.

Another approach to loving-kindness practice is to focus first on a person that you feel close to you. You imagine the person and then send thoughts such as:

May you be free from suffering.
May you be healthy.
May you be free from danger.
May you dwell in wisdom.
May you dwell in compassion.
May you rejoice in the happiness of others.

You can choose any words that you feel are appropriate. After focusing on someone you feel close to, you can choose someone who is more neutral in terms of your feeling. Again, imagine that person and repeat the words. Finally, you can pick a person you are having difficulty with or feel anger towards. This can be challenging and should not be undertaken if your negative emotions are still very strong.

Although this practice comes from the Buddhist tradition, I believe it is universal in nature. As I mentioned, I start my classes with the loving-kindness. I have had students from all the major faiths in my classes, and in my twenty-four years of using it in my class, no one has objected and felt they could not participate.

In the Buddhist teachings, the outcomes of loving-kindness practice include:

1 You will sleep easily.
2 You will wake easily.
3 You will have pleasant dreams.
4 People will love you.

5   Devas (celestial beings) and animals will love you.
6   Devas will protect you.
7   External dangers (poisons, weapons, and fire) will not harm you.
8   Your face will be radiant.
9   Your mind will be serene.
10 You will die unconfused.
11 You will be reborn in happy realms. (Salzberg 1995, 41)

Many of my students have reported a "more serene mind" and "sleeping more easily" after doing this practice. Research is now beginning on loving-kindness practice. It was found in one study that among university students who were taught this practice their kindness increased compared with a control group where their imagery was neutral (Hutcherson, Seppala, and Gross 2008).

Getting Started

If you have never meditated before, you may want to try the different methods for a while until you find the one you are most comfortable with. Again, the approach will probably be congruent with your orientation – intellectual, emotional, action, or physical. Once you have settled on an approach, stick with it. If you keep changing, your practice will probably not deepen.

To begin sitting meditation practice, sit comfortably with your head, neck, and chest in a straight line. You can sit in a chair or cross-legged on a cushion or bench. Most importantly, you should be in a position where you won't be shifting around a lot during the meditation. If you sit on a chair, choose a simple straight-backed chair where you can sit upright. Your feet should be on the floor; if they don't reach, put a cushion under your feet. The back should be straight. You should feel comfortable whatever position you take. It is also possible to meditate lying down, although there is the danger you may fall asleep. The eyes can be half-open looking softly down, or you can close them.

It is probably best to meditate at least one hour after eating. The times that seem to be most popular for meditation are early in the morning upon arising, before dinner, or late in the evening. You should choose a place free of distractions. If you have a room for meditation, fine; if not, then a corner of a bedroom can also be arranged so that it is conducive to meditation. Once you have settled on a time and place, others in the household should be made aware that you are not to be disturbed unless there is something urgent. However, you should not be unreasonable about your practice. For example, if there are young children in the household, you should probably not choose to meditate right before dinner, as this usually is a busy time around the household, and meditation practice could interfere with the needs of the family. Meditation should be done so that family life patterns are not drastically disturbed.

If you are just beginning practice and find it difficult, then just meditate for 5 to ten minutes. After a couple of weeks, you can gradually expand the time to twenty or thirty minutes. During meditation, you can look at your watch to check the time. Timers are also available, but it is perfectly all right to check a watch or clock during the meditation period. At the end, remain seated for a minute or two, thus allowing a space between the meditation and the resumption of daily activities.

The most important factor is daily practice. In my view, it is better to meditate ten minutes a day every day than to meditate for a longer period on an irregular basis. In the latter case, we can let things drift and end up not meditating at all.

Individuals who find it hard to keep a practice going find that sitting groups are helpful in maintaining practice. If there is not a sitting group in your area, you can try to start one. It is very helpful to do a retreat that can last from a weekend to several weeks as retreats can help deepen the practice.

Finally, it is helpful to have a teacher, particularly when you feel you find some difficulty in your practice. If you cannot find a teacher, then at least contact someone who has been meditating for a few years with whom you can talk about your practice. Ultimately, we must be the judge of our own practice.

Susan Moon (2010) had been doing Zen meditation most of her adult life. When a relationship broke up, she went into a deep depression. Her teachers continued to tell her that she should sit with the painful thoughts as they arise and pass away. However, she found if the painful thoughts passed away, they were only replaced by more painful thoughts. She was sitting in a retreat and finally decided to leave on the fifth day:

> I thought I had failed in my practice-decades of it! – and was bitterly disappointed in myself. Only later, after the depression subsided, did I see what a growth it was. Choosing not to sit was choosing not to be ruled by dogma, to be compassionate with myself, to take my spiritual practice into my own hands. (127)

Yes, the practice is ultimately in our own hands.

Activities That Support Our Practice

In this section, I outline some activities that can support our meditation practice and help us become contemplative practitioners. The contemplative life is ultimately a life of purpose, joy, and compassion. The contemplative life allows us to examine what is really important in life and so we are not pulled as much into pointless activity that tends to fragment and deaden our being.

Slowing Down

Our lives can be very hectic, almost frantic at times. We can feel that events have taken over as the pace of life seems to quicken with each year. We can find that our day can go something like this: We awaken each morning and, often, one of the first things that we do is turn on the radio or check the Internet to find out how the world made it through the night. Mornings can be very rushed as we get dressed, make breakfast, and help our children also get ready. We can often leave the house in the morning already feeling frazzled. As we commute to work, the drive can get our adrenalin pumping faster as the snarl of traffic can sometimes be overwhelming. As we arrive at work, we are often confronted with a long list of activities for the day that can involve meetings and encounters with others that can be stressful. At the end of the day, we can again face the problems of commuting as well as having to do errands on the way home. When we arrive home, there can be demands of family as well as the work of preparing and/or cleaning up the evening meal. The evenings can sometimes be filled with meetings, or work that we may have brought home. At the end of the day, we can feel exhausted. Although the weekends are supposed to be for relaxation, they can often be just as programmed as the weekday with jobs around the house, shopping, and social activities.

Carl Honore (2004) has written about the importance of slowness. In his book, he writes about the Slow Movement, which started with food and has spread to other areas, including education. Carlo Petrini, the founder of the slow food movement in Italy, believes that "being Slow means that you control the rhythms of your own life" (16). Slowing down, we start to do just one thing at time rather than trying to do several activities at once. We can build little gaps in the day. If we are driving or walking from one place to another, we can give ourselves extra time so that we can enjoy the drive or walk. By slowing down the pace of our lives, we can find a new source of energy as we feel less controlled by external events.

Slowing down does not mean becoming a zombie. Slowing down means approaching activities with freshness and focus. Mindfulness helps the whole process of slowing down as we bring our attention to our daily tasks, whatever they are.

Acceptance of Ambiguity and Imperfection

We live in a society where everything tends to be "managed." For years, our businesses and education systems have been run by management by objective. In contrast, other cultures are more comfortable with uncertainty and ambiguity. Richard Pascale and Anthony Athos (1981) have written about Japanese culture and have this to say:

> Ambiguity, uncertainty, and imperfection with their many shades of meaning, carry different connotations in the East than in the West. In the United States, for example, when a situation is "ambiguous," the implication is that it is incomplete, unstable, and needs clearing up. In Japan, in contrast, ambiguity is seen as having both desirable and undesirable aspects. The Japanese often seek a great deal of predictable order. But in other respects, having to do with many organizational matters, they are also willing to flow with things. More ambiguity, uncertainty, and imperfection in organizations is acceptable to them than to us as an immutable fact of life, what philosophers in the West have called "existential givens." By this they mean that such conditions just *are*, and, accordingly, the sooner we accept that they exist the better things will go. Regarding them as *enemies* gets our adrenalin pumping for a hopeless battle. Regarding them as conditions to be reduced or lived with as appropriate to the situation makes more sense. (141, original emphasis)

Ernest Kurtz and Katherine Ketcham (1992) write about the spirituality of imperfection, which is best seen in Alcoholics Anonymous (see chapter 5): "The spirituality of imperfection that forms the heart and soul of Alcoholics Anonymous makes no claim to be 'right.' It is a spirituality more interested in questions than answers, more a journey towards humility than a struggle for perfection" (5).

One area where we seem to have little tolerance for ambiguity is in the expectations we hold for other people. We can carry models in our head regarding how others should behave. We can become easily irritated by how people dress, speak, or walk. Ram Dass has noted that when we go into nature, we don't carry a model of how a tree or a flower should be.

We generally accept and even delight in the diversity of nature. Yet, with people, the least variation from our norms can make us annoyed. It is best to let go of these models we hold for others and for ourselves. Of course, we have expectations for people in our classrooms and the workplace, but I am not referring to these expectations. Instead, we often find ourselves becoming upset over superficial aspects of people's behaviour. Once, I was sitting in a meditation retreat and one of the participants had a cold and was coughing. His coughing upset me in my desire for "enlightenment." In time, I made a small change in my perspective and saw that this was just nature expressing itself through his cough. Seeing others as part of nature can help us feel free and at peace.

Mind the Gap

In our world, we seem almost compulsive in filling up the day so that there is very little free time. We can have little respect for the gaps or intervals in our lives. In contrast, the Japanese as well as other cultures accept the pauses and gaps. The Japanese, for example, call this space or interval, *ma*:

> Respect for *ma* deters us from plunging ahead when the right time for action is still impending. Gifted actors and comedians, great speakers and leaders, have an instinct for this quality. We have all noted the pause just prior to an important point when participants are momentarily waiting for release from tension created in part by the pause itself. But, as in theater, so also in organizational life, the magic fusion between anticipation and execution often fizzles. We have all witnessed a flow of organizational events building effectively toward closure only to see the overeager clumsily destroy consensus with a premature plunge toward the finish line. Such haste is as disastrous in organizations as in the theater. (Pascale and Athos, 1981, 144)

In traditional Japanese drawings, figures are usually placed within a large amount of space. The painting is not cluttered with too much detail, and we can find that the space can allow us to appreciate the drawing more.

Western culture is not comfortable with space or silence. For example, our homes tend to be filled with furniture and objects. We also find ourselves filling up silent moments with conversation, the radio, or television. I understand that in some Indigenous cultures an individual can enter another person's abode and stay there for a while without saying

anything and then get up and leave. Huston Smith (2009) tells the story
of when he said to his university class that his brother had suddenly died.
He made it through the class, but afterward one of the students, Douglas
George, a Native American, came with Smith to his office and sat with
him for twenty minutes of silence. Huston Smith found real comfort in
that silence (160).

From a contemplative perspective, we can appreciate the balance between silence/sound and space/figure. We learn how each is essential to
the other rather than having sound and material objects dominate.

Witnessing

Witnessing is another name for mindfulness. The witness is that place
in our consciousness that compassionately sees everything from a non-
judgmental perspective. The witness sees suffering and joy from a compassionate perspective that looks at the "tapes" that can take over our
lives. These are the tapes of addiction, compulsion, and other repeated
patterns. From the perspective of the witness, we can begin to see these
patterns more clearly and find that we do not immediately get caught up
in the tape.

For example, the witness can watch the patterns between ourselves and
others. If I find myself getting locked in arguments with my wife or child,
the compassionate witness can provide a place where I can see what is
happening. This perspective allows me to step back and not be so reactive
to everything that happens. I am not immediately drawn into the conflict.
Gradually, we may find that the pattern begins to loosen its hold. Yes, it
still may remain in some form, but the compulsion and rigidity associated
with the pattern are significantly diminished.

Nutrition/Exercise

We cannot ignore our bodies. Like everything else in our life, the body
needs to be honoured and respected. Through contemplation, we gradually witness what foods make us feel well and those foods that bring a
sense of heaviness. Gradually, our diets may change to foods that are
lighter. We eat less red meat and cut back on the fat in our diet. This
change in diet simply comes from seeing connections between foods and
how we feel. It does not come from reading about what we "should"
eat. In general, changes from meditation tend to arise gradually from
our awareness.

We may learn that we feel better if we exercise. The exercise does not have to be strenuous. Walking will do. Dean Ornish (1990) has found that meditation, a healthy diet, and exercise actually reverse the direction of heart disease. He has provided some striking evidence of how rather simple changes in our lifestyle can have profound effects on our health.

It is important that we not be compulsive about our food or diet or obsessive about slowing down. The contemplative approach to life involves a loosening up, not a tightening.

Humour

Humour helps us lighten up rather than tighten up. Humour is a wonderful source of healing and joy. The humour I am speaking of allows us to laugh at ourselves and with others rather than the forms of humour that exploit or categorize. We have evidence from people like Norman Cousins (2005) and Raymond Moody (1978) that laughter is good for us. The story of Norman Cousins is well known. When he heard he had a terminal illness, he took vitamin C and then started watching Marx Brothers films in his hospital room. He gradually got well through this therapy.

G.K. Chesterton said, "Angels can fly because they take themselves lightly." Humour helps in this process as it loosens the hold of the ego. It is so easy for us to get caught in our personal melodramas. Divorce, problems at work, or difficulties with our children can fill our minds with worry. It is helpful, then, to see our lives a part of the *lila*, or the dance or rhythm of life, rather than separating ourselves off with our own problems. Stephen Nachmanovitch (1990) describes *lila*:

> There is an old Sanskrit word, *lila*, which means play. Richer than our word, it means divine play, the play of creation, destruction and recreation, the folding and unfolding of the cosmos. *Lila*, free and deep, is both the delight and enjoyment of this moment, and the play of God. It also means love.
>
> *Lila* may be the simplest thing there is – spontaneous, childish, disarming. But as we grow and experience the complexities of life, it may also be the most difficult and hard-won achievement imaginable, and its coming to fruition is a kind of homecoming to our true selves. (1)

Music

Music and art can help our souls sing. Listening to music is particularly therapeutic. Like so many others, I find the music of Mozart very healing.

Here I would like to quote Jacques Lusseryan (1987) about the effects of music on his own being:

> The world of violins and flutes, of horns and cellos, of fugues, scherzos and gavottes, obeyed laws which were so beautiful and so clear that all music seemed to speak of God. My body was not listening, it was praying. My spirit no long had bounds, and if tears came to my yes, I did not feel them running down because they were outside me. I wept with gratitude every time the orchestra began to sing ...
>
> I loved Mozart so much, I loved Beethoven so much that in the end they made me what I am. They molded my emotions and guided my thoughts. Is there anything in me which I did not, one day, receive from them? I doubt it. (92–3)

Of course, the music does not have to be classical. Any music that touches the soul will do.

We need to sing more. The soul loves a good song, and when we sing the song our souls rejoice. Jack Kornfield (1993) tells a wonderful story about how a tribe in Africa connects each child with a song. When the mother wants to conceive a child with her mate, she goes and sits under a tree until she can hear the song of the child she hopes to conceive. Once she hears the song, she comes back to the village and shares it with her husband. They sing the song while they make love, thus hoping the child hears them. When the baby starts to grow in the womb, the mother sings the song to it along with other women in the village. Throughout labour and during birth, the baby is greeted by the song. Most of village learns the song so it can be sung to the child whenever he or she becomes hurt or is in danger. The song is also sung during various rituals in the child's life. The song is sung when the child marries. When the person is on her or his deathbed, friends and relatives gather to sing the song for the last time.

Journalling

There are many forms of journalling. In one of my classes, some students chose to keep a gratitude journal. Usually, this involves recording what we feel grateful for at the end of the day. One student, Sarah Truman, wrote that she started to experience gratitude as an embodied feeling:

> Over the first few weeks of the practice I noticed that gratitude is a feeling – a visceral feeling: I experience gratitude as an embodied sensation that is

warm and open at once. Once I recognized this aspect of gratitude, I could tell when I actually "felt" gratitude, from when I was just going through the motions of writing about something I "thought" I should feel grateful for.

Gradually, she began to notice the how this practice affected her life:

Over the first month, I noticed another change: similar to going to the gym, or being consistent with any practice, a transformation occurred. I noticed that I slipped into a "gratitude mood" more easily. Gratitude, and appreciative awareness became self-generating: as I practiced openness and gratitude daily, the more grateful and appreciative I became, and consequently I had more to feel "grateful" about.

All of the ideas and suggestions mentioned above could be used in ways that seem most appropriate. The idea is to employ these strategies in an organic manner rather than developing a formula. Patience is the key as we gradually develop our own approach to the contemplative life. I would like to quote Susan Moon (2010) again when she was depressed, "Choosing not to sit was choosing not to be ruled by dogma, to be compassionate with myself, to take my spiritual practice into my own hands" (127). At each step along the journey, we need to listen to ourselves and adjust our practice accordingly.

Chapter Four

Contemplatives and Their Practices

Perhaps the most powerful examples of contemplative practice come from individuals who made contemplation central to their spiritual lives. The lives and practices of these persons can inspire our own practice. The descriptions of contemplatives and their practices are brief here as the aim is to describe individuals from a variety of traditions. Eight individuals are discussed – Buddha, Rumi, Theresa of Avila, Emerson, Gandhi, Black Elk, Thomas Merton, and Aung San Suu Kyi.

Buddha

Although born almost 2,500 years ago, the Buddha and his teachings seem to be particularly relevant today. The Buddha asked that we simply observe our own experience in a wakeful manner. The Buddha's emphasis on spiritual practice based on watching our own personal experience seems particularly appropriate to our age. We have become suspicious of dogmas and rituals. In contrast, the Buddha avoided dogmatic assertion and encouraged each individual to be agent of his or her own awakening through mindfulness and meditation.

The Buddha, whose name was Siddhartha Gautama, was born in the sixth century BC in India. He was the son of a wealthy aristocrat who lived in northern India near what today is Nepal. His family was part of the aristocratic military class, which was equal in status to the priestly Brahmin class. Thus, Siddhartha grew up in very affluent surroundings. His father doted on his son and made sure that all of his son's needs were met; he also wanted his son protected from suffering and distress. Siddhartha's father forbade his son from leaving the palace grounds, because he did not want him to witness disease or death.

One of the main stories associated with the Buddha's youth is that he grew curious about what was outside the palace, and one day he left with his charioteer, Channa. When travelling around the city, he first saw an old man. He then saw a very sick person, and finally he saw a corpse.

Siddhartha began to reflect on how could anyone truly be happy if there was aging, sickness, and death. He asked people in the palace, but no one provided an adequate explanation. One day, outside the palace, he ran into a wandering holy man whose simple and calm presence suggested to him that what he needed to know was beyond the gates of the palace. He resolved to leave the palace in search of spiritual wisdom even though he was now married and had a young son. One night, he left the palace with Channa. Although, on the surface, leaving one's family appears cruel, most spiritual traditions indicate that, ultimately, we may have to put our spiritual quest above all other matters. For example, Christ indicated that his teachings could divide families. There is also a tradition in India that suggests that at some point in life (usually around age 40 or 50) it is acceptable to leave the family and devote oneself to the spiritual life.

The Buddha's first teacher was Alara Kalama, a hermit. But Kalama's teachings, although they were helpful, did not satisfy Siddhartha's deepest concerns. Siddhartha then entered a long period of extreme asceticism. For about six years, he fasted and meditated with five other seekers. Although Siddhartha learned to concentrate his mind during this period, he was not able to come to any understanding about age, sickness, and death. The fasting had also weakened him considerably. Siddhartha came then to the understanding that the body should not be abused in the search for spiritual understanding. He began taking food to restore his body. His five fellow seekers believed that the Buddha had given up the right way to enlightenment, so they left him.

Siddhartha, after nourishing himself, now began his famous meditation under the Bodhi tree, which was located in what today is the town of Bodhgaya in India. Siddhartha was around thirty years of age. When he began his meditation, a young woman named Sujata brought him a bowl of rice milk. According to one story, Siddhartha drank from the bowl and then placed the golden bowl in a river where it proceeded to float upstream against the current. The bowl came to rest in front of the place where the Serpent King lived. This story metaphorically represents Buddhism's relation to nature since the Serpent King signifies the wisdom of nature. Other stories concerning the Buddha's life also show the connection between his teachings and the natural world. As we struggle to overcome the environmental degradation of this age, such stories take on added significance.

Joseph Campbell (1949) summarizes Siddhartha's experience under the tree and confrontation with the god, Mara:

> The dangerous god appeared mounted on an elephant and carrying weapons in his thousand hands. He was surrounded by his army, which extended twelve leagues before him, twelve to the right, twelve to the left, and in the rear as far as to the confines of the world; it was nine leagues high. The protecting deities of the universe took flight, but the Future Buddha remained unmoved beneath the Tree. And the god then assailed him, seeking to break his concentration.
>
> Whirlwind, rocks, thunder and flame, smoking weapons with keen edges, burning coals, hot ashes, boiling mud, blistering sands and fourfold darkness, the Antagonist hurled against the Savior, but the missiles were all transformed into celestial flowers and ointments by the power of Gautama's ten perfections. Mara then deployed his daughters, Desire, Pining, and Lust, surrounded by voluptuous attendants, but the mind of the Great Being was not distracted. The god finally challenged his right to be sitting on the Immovable Spot, flung his razor-sharp discus angrily and bid the towering host of the army to let fly at him with mountain crags. But the future Buddha only moved his hand to touch the ground with his fingertips, and thus bid the goddess Earth bear witness to his right to be sitting where he was. She did so with a hundred, a thousand, a hundred thousand roars, so that the elephant of the Antagonist fell upon its knees in obeisance to the Future Buddha. The army was immediately dispersed and the gods of all the worlds scattered garlands. (32)

Again, this story signifies basic elements in Buddhism and Buddhist practice. For example, when the Buddha points to the earth, he suggests that the primary witness to his enlightenment is the Earth itself. In a sense, the Buddha grounds his spiritual awakening in the Earth. The story is also a metaphor for our own struggle to meditate and to concentrate the mind in spite of desire and other forms of restlessness. The Buddha's enlightenment is the great event in Buddhism where he gained understandings that were later expressed in the four noble truths and the eightfold path.

The Buddha maintained that each of us can attain enlightenment through meditative practice. Enlightenment is not something that is separate or remote but available to us in the here-and-now. Central to this experience of enlightenment is witnessing the interdependence of all matter and energy. The Buddha saw very clearly how all things arise and then pass away in a deep and connected way.

After this experience, the Buddha decided that he must share his understanding with others on earth. The Buddha had attained nirvana and could have remained detached from human striving, but instead, out of infinite compassion for all beings, he taught and shared his discoveries with others. The decision to teach and serve, even though one has attained enlightenment, is at the centre of the *bodhisattva* tradition in Buddhism. The bodhisattva defers his or her own nirvana until all beings have attained liberation. Central to Buddhism, then, is compassion. Compassion arises from understanding, at the deepest level, that all is connected and that separation from others is an illusion.

The Buddha began his teaching by returning to his former companions. They were struck by the Buddha's radiance and were drawn to him immediately and he began teaching them. He shared the four noble truths that include:

1 Suffering is inherent in existence.
2 Suffering and dissatisfaction arise from our grasping and our sense of separateness (e.g., the ego).
3 We can let go of our grasping and sense of separation.
4 The release from ego and greed can occur through the eightfold path.

The eightfold path involves:

1 Right understanding
2 Right purpose
3 Right speech
4 Right conduct
5 Right livelihood
6 Right effort
7 Right awareness
8 Right concentration, or meditation.

Right understanding refers to witnessing the four noble truths. *Right purpose* involves a sense that we are on a path and are committed to spiritual practice. *Right speech* and *conduct* mean that we do not intentionally harm others by speech or action. *Right livelihood* suggests that our work should not involve any activity that would harm others or contribute to their suffering. *Right effort* refers to the fact that each of us must make an individual effort to awaken. *Right awareness* means that in our daily actions we are mindful or fully present. Finally, we need to *contemplate and concentrate* the mind through meditative practice.

Through his teachings and presence, the Buddha inspired his followers to become monks and to go out into the world to teach. The monks approached teaching not as proselytizing but simply through the example of their own practice. The Buddha also encouraged his followers not to engage in intellectual or theoretical debates. He felt that intellectual exchanges sidetrack us from our path to wisdom and compassion. Garma C.C. Chang explains:

> Buddha was never [merely] a philosopher: His primary concern was to point out the way to liberation – liberation from the deep-rooted attachment to a delusory self which is the source of all passion-desires and their resultant pains and frustrations. Philosophical speculations were persistently rejected and denounced by Buddha as useless, foolish and unsalutary. Actually, in Buddha's teaching we do not find a philosophy; what we find is a significant therapeutic device, the instruction on how to get rid of the deep ego-clinging attitude. (Cited in Ross 1980, 28)

Central to Buddhism is the connection between thought and action. Through meditation and mindfulness, we begin to root out inconsistencies between thought and action. By seeing connections at all levels, we begin to live more in harmony with the basic teachings so that they become living reality. The following Buddhist saying captures this idea very well:

> The thought manifests as the word,
> The word manifests as the deed,
> The deed develops into habit,
> And the habit hardens into character.
> So watch the thought
> And its way with care,
> And let it spring from love
> Born out of respect for all beings.

By witnessing how our thoughts give rise to certain actions, simple attention to this process can free us and make us more compassionate. This process of meditation and mindfully watching our thoughts and actions is an organic one. We are not imposing a set of beliefs on ourselves or others, we are simply trying to *see*, or to be fully awake. This process leads to a gradual unfolding or flowering of what Buddhists call the *dharma*, or the truth or law underlying all things.

The Buddha taught for almost fifty years. In that time, he taught all manner of people and accepted women into the order of monks. He did return to his home so he could share his teachings with his father, wife, and son.

The Buddha died when he was about eighty years old. The Buddha still taught as he neared his death. He told his disciples, "Work with diligence. Be lamps unto yourselves. Betake yourselves to no external refuge. Look not for refuge to anyone beside yourself. Hold fast to the truth as to a lamp."

Rumi

Rumi lived in the thirteenth century (1207–1273) and is considered one of the greatest mystic poets. In the Muslim world, Rumi is known as Jalal ad-Din Muhammad Balkhi, and he was born in the village of Vakhsh, now part of Tajikistan. His father, Baha al-Din, was a scholar and eventually headed a *madrases*, a religious school. Rumi spent most of his life in the town of Konya, which now lies in Turkey. Rumi was married twice and had three children. One of his sons, Sultan Walad, helped organize the Mevlevi order; the practices of the Mevlevi are based on Rumi's teachings and include the dances of the Whirling Dervishes. Rumi was an observant Muslim and upheld the five pillars of Islam that include praying five times a day, fasting during Ramadan, and making the pilgrimage to Mecca. Rumi was a Sufi, a mystical sect of Islam that focuses on the inner life as central to spiritual growth.

For many years, Rumi was a scholar and teacher, but his life changed when he met his teacher Shams-e Tabrizi, in 1244. As a teacher, Rumi had many followers. When Shams came to Konya, Rumi spent a most of his time with his new teacher. Rumi's students were jealous of Shams, and this caused Shams to leave Konya twice. The second time Shams left, in 1246, he did not return and died soon after leaving Konya.

Shams was a mystic. He asked people to reflect on these questions, "Who am I, and what is my essence? And to what end have I come here and where am I headed and what are my roots and what am I doing this very hour and what is my focus?" (cited in Lewis 2008, 143).

Rumi's separation from Shams led to intense and painful grieving. The whole experience of being with Shams and the eventual separation led to Rumi's famous poetry. Much of this poetry is in the *Masnavi*, which contains 2,700 lines of Persian poetry. Rumi's contemplative path was one of love of the divine; the ultimate goal was union with God. The knowledge that results from this union is *Kibriya*, which means Divine Glory. This vision of Kibriya is one of joy, adoration, and love. Andrew Harvey (1994) writes that Rumi is "the supreme guide on the Path of Love for the human race" (50). Like many mystics, Rumi believed that love is at the centre of the universe. Franklin Lewis (2008), in his biography, writes that Rumi believed "love is at the root of the outward aspect of the things we see in this world. Love gives rise to the multiplicity of forms, but these are secondary and non-essential" (406). Rumi, in a line similar to Dante's last lines in the *Divine Comedy*, tells us, "It's waves of love that make the heavens turn" (cited in Lewis, 417).

Harvey (1994) describes three stages in Rumi's contemplative process that lead to the third and final stage of union. The first stage is *purification*, which involves a commitment to a spiritual discipline or, in Harvey's words, "a housecleaning" (82). Shunryu Suzuki Roshi (1970), also stated that we need to have a house cleaning of our minds:

So we say true understanding will come out of emptiness. When you study Buddhism, you have a general house cleaning of your mind. You must take everything out of your room and clean it thoroughly ...

One after another you will have thoughts in your mind, but if you want to stop your thinking you can ... But as long as you have some fixed idea or are caught by some habitual way of doing things, you cannot appreciate things in their true sense. (112)

Emptying the mind has been central to most spiritual traditions. Angelus Silesius, a Renaissance Christian mystic, explained:

God whose love and joy are everywhere
Can't come to visit
Unless you aren't there. (Cited in Kornfield 1993, 74)

After purification, the next stage for Rumi was *expansion*. Harvey (1994) writes:

Sufis make the distinction, a subtle distinction, between what they call *hal* and *maqam*. *Hal* refers to the Divine states, moments of bliss, visions, dreams, sudden ecstasies. These are states that come and go. *Maqam* are stations ... stations you acquire by work, by mystical work, inner work and transformation. (83)

This stage involves a radical opening of the heart, which happened for Rumi with Shams. The heart becomes so open that Divine can take root. It allows for the final stage of union, called *baqa*, "an endless experience of bliss and joy, an endless theophany" (84). Rumi writes (103):

My soul is flooded by your Sea of splendor,
Being and cosmos drown there silently.

For Rumi, like for so many contemplatives, silence was central to the experience of union. Rumi teaches (122):

Keep silent, because the world of silence is a vast fullness.
Do not beat the drum of words. The word is only an empty drum.

Rumi, who could use words so beautifully, knew that all words arise out of the great silence: "No more words, hear only the voice within" (129). Only in silence can the still small voice within be heard.

Gandhi (1999) also referred to this voice: "There are moments in your life when you must act, even though you cannot carry your best friends with you. The 'still small voice' within you must always be the final arbiter when there is conflict of duty" (62).

Sufis are known for dance, more specifically the dance of the Whirling Dervishes. This dance, or *sama*, is an expression of divine union and even of the cosmos itself. Harvey (1994) describes the philosophy underlying this dance: The dancers are dressed in white and black representing "death to the world and death to desire" (242). At the centre is the sheik, representing Rumi, as well as the intersection between time and the timeless. The sheik sits on a red carpet; red being the colour of sky in Konya when Rumi was dying and "entering the final union with the Beloved" (ibid.). Next, a singer begins with a text written by Rumi praising the Prophet, Mohammed. Drumming also begins as the sheik taps the rhythm. A flute starts playing and improvising. With the music, the dancers start moving slowly. The sheik stands and the dancers bow to the sheik and begin to dance. The left hand of each dancer is turned to heaven while the right hand is turned down to steer the divine energy to the earth. The dancers represent the unity and multiplicity in the cosmos.

The dancing is symbolic on many levels as the sheik also represents the sun with dancers being the circling planets. The sun is an image that runs throughout Rumi's poetry and the name, Shams, actually means sun. Towards the end of the dancing, the flute plays again. According to Harvey, "this moment, when the flute reenters, is considered the supreme moment, the moment of deep union with God" (244). When the dancing stops, the singer sings verses from the Koran; then there is silence, followed by the chanting of the *dikhr*.

For Rumi, contemplation was closely linked to the arts – poetry, dance, and music; the Whirling Dervish finds union through the music and dance. Many of Rumi's poems were written when he was dancing. He wanted those who read his poetry also to dance, "I have not sung the *Masnavi* for you to hold it or repeat it, but to put it under you feet, so you could fly" (cited in Harvey 1994, 246).

Saint Teresa of Avila

Teresa of Avila lived in sixteenth-century Spain. Although Teresa was Catholic, her father came from Jewish ancestry. He married twice, as his first wife died after having two children; his second wife had eight children including seven boys. Teresa was the eldest and helped with raising the boys. However, around age twenty, she decided to join a convent. She chose the Incarnation order, which was more relaxed than many other orders.

The Incarnation convent in Avila was crowded, with about two hundred women living within its walls. It was open to visitors who might bring food or gifts to the nuns, and these visitors included men who sometimes flirted with the nuns. By all accounts, Teresa was beautiful, and the men who came to the convent were immediately attracted to her. Eventually, she found the male company such a distraction to her vocation that she became sick. Thus, she went back home to recover. While at home, she read *The Third Spiritual Alphabet*, by Francisco de Osuna. This book introduced Teresa to contemplative prayer and provided the initial impetus to her contemplative practice. Teresa was sick for two years, and at one point she was so ill that she almost died.

Teresa returned to the convent and found that she was subject to the same temptations. She still found herself holding court in the parlour of the convent. Again, there were many male visitors, and apparently one, who has remained nameless, attracted her attention and affections. She struggled with her conflicts for many years, until she was forty. At that time, she experienced a second spiritual rebirth, the first being her sickness and recovery when she was in her early twenties. Carol Lee Flinders (1993) describes this event:

> One minute Teresa was walking past an image of the crucified Christ recently placed in a corridor of the Incarnation, and the next, they tell us, she was on her knees, sobbing, repenting of nearly twenty years' indifference, and begging God to strengthen her once and for all. In truth, this sudden conversion had been a long time in the making. (169)

Flinders explains that this conversion was the result of years of contemplative prayer in which Teresa would begin the time of prayer feeling conflicted, but at the end would say, in her own words, that she felt a "greater quiet and delight."

At the same time, someone gave Teresa a copy of St. Augustine's *Confessions*, and she wept when she read it. Teresa found Augustine's spiritual path similar to her own. His narrative inspired her contemplation, much as *The Spiritual Alphabet* had done twenty years earlier.

The parlour was no longer a threat to her spiritual life as she found that her contemplation deepened and that she could communicate with God as an intimate friend: " No longer do I want you to converse with men, but with angels" (Theresa of Avila 1946, vol. 1, 155).

Through contemplation, Teresa seemed to find a deeper spiritual voice. Teresa travelled from the convent in Avila to found seventeen Carmelite convents and four monasteries. She travelled all over Spain in a donkey cart. The efforts in each community to establish a convent were not always well received, but Teresa's powerful presence helped forge the establishment of each convent. Once established, the convents were often fraught with conflicts between the nuns, and she had to resolve the problems through letters or a personal visit. All these problems contributed to her declining health that included arthritis, heart disease, malaria, and a broken shoulder that was never properly set and gave her constant pain. Despite these difficulties, her literary output was tremendous during this whole period. She was ordered to write her *Autobiography* in order to make her contemplative prayer clear to others. This was the period of the Inquisition, and ecstatic contemplative states were well known and often seen as heretical. The Dominicans, who ran the Inquisition, were suspicious of silent prayer.

Teresa's contemporaries claimed that her writing was much like her speech. Although it tended to wander, it was invariably direct and accessible; she was able to develop her own voice. She did not try to emulate the learned style of the Dominicans but instead adopted vernacular that disarmed her opposition (Flinders 1993, 176). Teresa's writing was filled with images. She referred to one hermit saint who was made of "nothing but tree roots." She wrote about the challenges of meditation in a manner that is understandable to any meditator, no matter what tradition that person comes from, saying, "This intellect is so wild that it doesn't seem to be anything else than a frantic madman no one can tie down" (177).

In the *Autobiography*, Teresa describes the stages of mental prayer as the "four waters," and each of these stages refers to how one waters a garden. The first water is drawn from the well and requires determined effort. The main challenge at this beginning stage is distractedness, and the essential aspect of contemplative practice is simply determination.

The second stage refers to a system of aqueducts and a waterwheel whose crank must be turned. Less effort is now required than in the first stage, as one begins to experience grace, which allows one to be "nearer the light."

The third stage is characterized by a river or spring. Our task here is to direct the flow of the river, and this becomes more effortless as we align ourselves with God. We experience more joy and delight at this stage.

The final stage is where we experience union with God. The metaphor that Teresa (1946) uses here is one of rainfall: "This rain comes from Heaven to fill and saturate the whole of this garden" (vol. 1, 108). This union, however, is not ethereal or divorced from our humanity: "It is an important thing that while we are living and are human we have human support" (ibid.). She also felt that the body should not be denied or abused.

Teresa's writing (1946) was much like the water she describes; it simply flowed: "I realize clearly that it is not I who am saying this; for I am not putting it together with my own understanding and afterwards I cannot tell how I managed to say it all" (vol. 1, 86).

Teresa's next book was *The Way of Perfection*, which also describes the contemplative life. Before one approaches contemplative practice, she teaches, there must be love, detachment, and humility. For Teresa, love is best seen as spiritual friendship, where we share a concern for the other person's spiritual growth. Detachment means that we are not overly involved with others or the petty things in life. Seeing things from a larger perspective, we develop "freedom of spirit" (cited in Flinders 1993, 183). Humility involves not making excuses for oneself. Teresa refers particularly to her own life and how her friend, St. John of the Cross, told her one day, "You have a fine way of excusing yourself" (ibid.). Teresa stresses the qualities of love, detachment, and humility because the environment in which one practises contemplation is as important as the meditation itself. When these qualities are absent, then contemplation is much more difficult to practise.

In *The Way of Perfection*, Teresa argues for the value of silent prayer. She believes that within each person is "an extremely rich palace, built entirely of gold and precious stones" (Flinders 1993, 184). It is difficult to access this palace, and Teresa (1946) makes particular reference to women: "For, as we women are not learned, or fine witted, we need all things to help us realize that we actually have something within us incomparably more precious than anything we see outside" (vol. 2, 117).

Teresa often addresses women in her work, and she never wavers in her assumption that contemplative prayer is the birthright of women as well as men" (Flinders 1993, 184).

Teresa's third major work, *Interior Castle*, was written when she was sixty-two. She starts this book with the following lines: "I began to think of the soul as if it were a castle made out of a single diamond or of very clear crystal, in which there are many rooms" (vol. 2, 201). In this book, she describes seven stages of contemplation. The first three stages have to do with settling down, while the fourth stage is a transition period from the natural to the supernatural. The fifth stage is where one finds union and is born into a new life with Christ. Here Teresa uses the metaphor of a silkworm, describing how the soul dies in the cocoon and is transformed into a white butterfly. The sixth stage can be a long period where the person experiences further trials to prepare for the final stage. The final stage she finds difficult to describe; she says she may not have fully realized this dimension of spiritual life. Nevertheless, she describes the last stage as a life with Christ where we experience limitless love.

Teresa's struggles were many as she travelled across Spain setting up new convents. Flinders (1993) compares her approach to the work of Gandhi, who had the ability to find common ground with others and to compromise:

> Teresa operated in much the same way, drawing to her cause and into her affections individuals who did not always seem worthy of that honor. She did so for the same reason Gandhi would: the work at hand was far too urgent to be postponed until perfect men and women came along to undertake it. (89)

Teresa of Avila is an example of someone who combined contemplation and action in powerful ways. She shows that the contemplative life is a powerful source of acting creatively in the world.

Emerson

Ralph Waldo Emerson is widely studied and quoted today. The Afro-American scholar Charles Johnson (2003) in his introduction to Emerson's writings states:

> His catholicity – as a standard and challenge – inspires even today, as does his devotion to Reason, which placed him, happily, on the right side of history as a spirited nonconformist, who championed the right of women to vote; who passionately spoke out against slavery in such addresses as "Emancipation in the British West Indies," against the evil of the Fugitive Slave Act, which turned "all the Citizens of this hemisphere into kidnappers," against the "wicked Indian policy"; and who wrestled with the received idea, so common at the time, of the supposed inferiority of blacks. (x)

Thomas Moore (2002), who through his extensive writings has restored the word "soul" to the contemporary context, writes that Emerson "represents the best in the spiritual explorer. I can't read enough by him or about him" (74).

Emerson's appeal lies, in part, because he called on the individual to trust his or her own powers, particularly the intuitive sense. Emerson (2003) wrote, "Insist on yourself, never imitate" (268): "Nothing is sacred except the integrity of your own mind" (269). Silence and solitude are important to release our intuitive powers: "It is easy in the world to live after the world's opinions; it is easy in solitude to live after our own" (271). In solitude, the "mind is simple" and receives divine wisdom. It is empty and through this emptiness wisdom can arise. Emerson calls the wisdom that arises in this way "Intuition." This is a place where "analysis cannot go" and comes from a place where "all life and being" proceed (277). Emerson read extensively and integrated this reading into his work; however, he felt the primary inspirational source was the "infinitude" within each person.

Another reason for the interest in Emerson lies simply with the man himself. Oliver Wendell Holmes (1980), a contemporary of Emerson and a critic of his mysticism, nevertheless said the following in his book *Ralph Waldo Emerson*:

Judged by his life, Emerson comes very near our best ideal of humanity. No matter of what he wrote or spoke, his words, his tones, his looks, carried the evidence of a sincerity which pervaded them all and was to his eloquence and poetry like the water of crystallization; without which they would effloresce into mere rhetoric ...

There are living organisms so transparent that we can see their hearts beating and their blood flowing through their glassy tissues. So transparent was the life of Emerson; so clearly did the true nature of the man show through it. What he taught others to be, he was himself. His deep and sweet humanity won him love and reverence everywhere among those whose natures were capable of responding to the highest manifestations of character. (324–5)

Emerson's thinking, writing, and life were integrated. It is this integration of his work and thought that is so appealing. It is not just his writing that strikes a responsive chord today, but the authenticity of the man himself.

Ralph Waldo Emerson was born on 25 May 1803, in Boston, Massachusetts. His father, who was a minister, died when Emerson was eight years old. His mother managed to support the family so that Emerson and his brothers could go to school. Emerson studied at Harvard and he, too, became a minister. He married shortly after beginning his Unitarian ministry, but his first wife died of tuberculosis less than eighteen months later. Emerson was to suffer many personal tragedies in his life, including the death of a son; however, these events did not alter his optimistic philosophy or his humane disposition.

After the death of his first wife, Emerson examined his religious beliefs and resigned from his ministerial post in Boston. He felt that the rituals of organized religion tended to ossify the individual's direct contact with God. Thus, he began the career as lecturer and writer that was to continue for the rest of his life. In both the United States and England, he was known as the foremost lecturer of the nineteenth century. John Trowbridge said, "Emerson was no orator ... he had no gift of extempory utterance, no outburst of improvisation. But in the expression of ethical thought, or in downright moral vehemence, I believed and still believe him unequaled" (McAleer 1984, 493). James Russell Lowell agreed: "I have heard some great speakers and some accomplished orators, but never any that so moved and persuaded me as he" (cited in ibid.).

Moncure Conway has said that Emerson's address at Harvard Divinity School in 1838 "stands in the moral history of America where the Declaration of Independence stands in its political history" (cited in

McAleer 1984, 248–9). This address met with a harsh reaction as Emerson questioned the tenets of traditional Christianity. He began the address by arguing that within each person is a "religious sentiment" that exists within the soul. It seeks beauty, truth, and love. This sentiment is the divine in the human being, and problems arise when institutions such as the Church deny this sentiment and, instead, focus on external authority. Emerson (2003) felt that we must find the Christ within rather than look to the doctrines and rituals of the Church: "Dare to love God without mediator or veil" (261). Emerson's talk was met with anger, and he was not invited to speak at Harvard for several decades.

Although Emerson did not like the term "transcendentalist," he was considered part of the group identified by that name. Transcendentalists argued that individuals are most capable of moral behaviour when they are in touch with their own conscience or that "still small voice within." The transcendentalists included – among others – Margaret Fuller, Bronson Alcott, and Henry David Thoreau. Emerson was mentor to these individuals, particularly to Thoreau, who also lived in Concord. Emerson encouraged Thoreau in his Walden venture.

Although Emerson was not a social activist, he was willing to take a stand regarding critical social issues. He spoke out against slavery and opposed the expulsion of the Cherokee Indians from Georgia. He was supportive of women's rights. Although he was capable of deep moral indignation, he abhorred fanaticism and always worked from the "deep humanity" that Holmes and others witnessed.

Emerson lived most of his life in Concord, Massachusetts, with his second wife, Lidian. Emerson was deeply loved by those who knew him. Late in his life, his house burned and the citizens of Concord had his home rebuilt while Emerson travelled. He died in 1882.

Emerson (2003) was not a rigorous philosopher who developed a comprehensive philosophical system. In fact, he coined the phrase "a foolish consistency is the hobgoblin of little minds" (273). He was an eclectic, and he drew on many sources. In particular, he was influenced by Plato and Neoplatonists such as Plotinus and by Goethe. He saw the inadequacy of empiricism as expressed by Locke and Hume. He felt that empiricism, with its emphasis on sensation, limits the individual's capacity for moral imagination. Emerson believed that the individual and the universe were connected through a fundamental unity:

> In the woods, we return to reason and faith. There I feel that nothing can befall me in life – no disgrace, no calamity (leaving me my eyes), which nature cannot repair. Standing on the bare ground – my head bathed by the

blithe air, and uplifted into infinite space – all mean egotism vanishes. I become a transparent eyeball; I am nothing; I see all; the currents of the Universal Being circulate through me; I am part or particle of God. (184)

We are able to see or apprehend this unity not by sensation but through intuition. According to Emerson (2003):

The inquiry leads us to that source, at once the essence of genius, of virtue, and of life, which we call Spontaneity or Instinct. We denote this primary wisdom as Intuition, whilst all later teachings are tuitions. In that deep force, the last fact behind which analysis cannot go, all things find their common origin. (267)

How do we develop this intuition? Emerson believed in the value of silent contemplation. He liked to take long walks on the trails surrounding Concord. He would then return to his study and record his thoughts. Emerson kept a journal, the primary source for his lectures and essays. By the end of his life, his journals and note taking totalled 230 volumes.

For Emerson, consciousness was primary and he sought to deepen it through meditation and reflection. He looked forward to the time of "self-union" where he was alone and could simply be with nature and his own thoughts. Emerson (2003), like most contemplatives, focused on being in the present moment:

In nature every moment is new; the past is always swallowed and forgotten; the coming only is sacred [323] ... Whenever a mind is simple and receives a divine wisdom, old things pass away, – it lives now and absorbs past and future into the present hour [278] ... Five minutes of to-day are worth as much time as five minutes in the next millennium. Let us be poised, and wise, and our own, to-day. (359)

Emerson felt that by emptying ourselves we then see the truth behind the images of things. He was deeply influenced by Plato, and he felt that behind the physical world lay a more perfect spiritual world where the essence of things lay. Through solitude and quiet we can gain access to this invisible world, the Over-Soul (see chapter 5). However, Emerson does not create a duality between the physical and non-visible worlds. The beauty of nature is the external representation of the beauty of the soul:

In the tranquil landscape, and especially in the distant line of the horizon, man beholds somewhat as beautiful as his own nature.

> The greatest delight which the fields and woods minister, is the suggestion of an occult relation between man and the vegetable. I am not alone and unacknowledged. They nod to me, and I to them ...
>
> Yet it is certain that the power to produce this delight does not reside in nature, but in man, or in a harmony of both. (185)

According to Gay Wilson Allen (1981), Emerson also anticipated thinkers like Fritjof Capra with his insights into nature as Emerson saw a connection between matter and energy:

> There is one animal, one planet, one matter and one force that is, [energy]. The laws of light and of heat translate into each other; so do the laws of sound and of color; and so galvanism, electricity, and magnetism are varied forms of the self-same energy. While the student ponders this immense unity, he observes that all things in nature, the animals, the mountain, the river, the seasons, wood, iron, stone, vapor, have a mysterious relation to his thoughts and his life; their growths, decays, quality, and use so curiously resemble himself in parts and in wholes that he is compelled to speak by means of them. (576)

For Emerson, we are not separate from nature but are deeply connected.

Of the contemplatives mentioned in this chapter, Emerson is the classic householder. With his wife, Lidian, he raised three children, lived in one community his whole life, and made his living by writing and lecturing. He served on the Concord school board and attended town meetings. In short, he did not separate himself from society. Yes, he withdrew to the woods to contemplate and reflect but always returning to write down his thoughts, which he then shared in his lectures.

Emerson's neighbours in Concord enjoyed his presence. The author Nathaniel Hawthorne, who was not a close friend, once said in speaking of Emerson, "a pure intellectual gleam diffused about his presence like the garment of a shining one" (cited in McAleer 1984, 102). Hawthorne's wife, Sophia, said this:

> It became one of my happiest experiences to pass Emerson upon the street. Yet, I caviled at his self-consciousness, his perpetual smile. I complained that he ought to wait for something to smile at. After a time, I realized that he always had something to smile FOR, if not to smile AT; and that a cheerful countenance is heroic. By and by I learned that he always could find something to smile at also; for he tells us, "The best of all jokes is the sympathetic contemplation of things." (Cited in Holmes 1980, 238–9)

In Buddhism, there is the concept of sympathetic joy where we derive happiness from the joy of others. Emerson apparently had this quality. Emerson's presence is also described by the famous Harvard professor, Charles Eliot Norton. Norton was returning to the United States from Europe just after his wife had died and he was quite depressed. Emerson, who was seventy years old at the time, was on the same ship, and the two spent much time together. Initially, Norton was put off by Emerson's optimism. Shortly after the trip, however, he wrote his friend James Russell Lowell, "Emerson made the voyage pleasant to me. He had a spirit of perennial youthfulness. He is the youngest man I know" (cited in McAleer 1984, 623). In 1903 Norton paid a centennial tribute to Emerson when he said that Emerson was one of the most important teachers in his life.

Emerson, then, had the elusive quality of presence, we might even say, a loving presence. In one essay on education, Emerson (2003) speaks to teachers and talks about this quality:

> To whatsoever upright mind, to whatsoever beating heart I speak, to you it is committed to educate men. By simple living, by an illimitable soul, you inspire, you correct, you instruct, you raise, you embellish all ... The beautiful nature of the world has here blended your happiness with your power. Work straight on in absolute duty, and you lend an arm and an encouragement to all the youth of the universe. Consent yourself to be an organ of your highest thought, and lo! suddenly you put all men in your debt, and are the fountain of an energy that goes pulsing on waves of benefit to the borders of society, to the circumference of things. (484–5)

Although he is speaking to teachers, Emerson's words describe his own power as a teacher. His energy, like all great teachers', is still "pulsing to the circumference of things."

Gandhi

Gandhi is an outstanding example of a contemplative involved in social action. Gandhi did not separate his "spiritual" life from his political activity; for him, it was all connected. Gandhi said, "My life is an indivisible whole, and all my activities run into one another" (cited in Easwaran 1978, 5).

Gandhi was born on 2 October 1869, in Porbandar, a small, seaside town in western India. His father, Karamchand Gandhi, was a politician who served as prime minister to the raja in the small domains near

Porbandar. His mother, Putlibai, was a devout Hindu whom Gandhi remembered as a deeply religious person.

As a boy, Gandhi was not exceptional except that he was extremely shy. Gandhi, like most Indians, was married at a very early age: at age thirteen he married Kasturbai. In his youth, he was quite a demanding husband and the two often fought. However, the marriage endured, due mainly to her patience, forbearance, and strong will. At the beginning of the marriage he saw himself as her teacher, but as the years passed her strength, courage, and patience became a strong example to him and influenced him in the development of *satyagraha* (soul-force), which was his approach to non-violent change.

Gandhi did not do well in school. After high school, he went to college but dropped out after five months. Gandhi's uncle suggested that he go to London to study law, and Gandhi spent three years there where he attained his law degree. When he returned to India, he was devastated to learn that his mother had died. He also could not find work as a lawyer as he knew nothing of Indian law and was still very shy. On his first case, he got up to cross-examine a witness and he could not utter a single word; he was called by his colleagues the "briefless barrister."

A major turning point in Gandhi's life was when he began legal work in South Africa. On his first train ride, in South Africa, his law firm had reserved him a first class ticket. In the evening, a white passenger came into his compartment and objected to the presence of a dark-skinned Indian. When the train officials asked Gandhi to move to the third class section, he refused to do so. He was thrown off the train at the next stop, and he had to spend the cold night at the station. During that evening, Gandhi thought about returning to India but decided that he must stay. Later, Gandhi would refer to this incident as the most creative moment in his life. He decided that long night in the train station that he would never yield to force, nor would he use force to achieve an end. This was the seed that developed into satyagraha.

In South Africa, Gandhi was first asked to help with a complicated case, which required knowledge of accounting. Gandhi applied himself and was able to attain an out-of-court settlement. He said, "I had learnt to find out the better side of human nature and to enter men's hearts. I realized that the true function of a lawyer was to unite parties riven asunder" (cited in Easwaran 1978, 22). Gandhi's first success led to others, and he became well established as a lawyer. However, after several years there, Gandhi became involved in relieving the suffering of the Indians who lived in South Africa. These people worked as labourers in situations equivalent to slavery. As he witnessed and helped these people, he began to simplify his life; he gave up the expensive clothes and made his household simple. At first, he tried to impose this new life on his wife, Kasturbai, who resisted. Her resistance led Gandhi to an important insight: in order to change others you must first change yourself. Gandhi realized leadership must come from example.

The *Bhagavad Gita* was another powerful influence for Gandhi. He read it daily, it became his guide for living. He said, "To me the Gita became an infallible guide of conduct. It became my dictionary of daily reference" (cited in Easwaran 1978, 35). The *Gita* also inspired Gandhi to meditate. For the rest of his life, he would rise around four and meditate in the quiet of the early morning.

In 1906, thirteen years after Gandhi's arrival in South Africa, the white government of Transvaal introduced legislation to take away the few rights that the Indians held in South Africa. Gandhi strongly opposed the measure and proposed to a crowd that they resist the legislation in a non-violent manner. He advocated civil disobedience:

Civil disobedience is the inherent right of a citizen. Disobedience must be sincere, respectful, restrained, never defiant, must be based upon some well-understood principle, must not be capricious, and above all, must not have ill will or hatred behind it. (Cited in Easwaran 1978, 43)

Satyagraha means "holding on to truth" or "soul-force." Truth, for Gandhi, was eternal and unchangeable, while evil and injustice exist only with our support. Once we agree to hold to the truth, we become free. Freedom starts in our own hearts and minds, and satyagraha is based on individual and collective commitment to holding to truth. *Ahisma*, or non-violence, was the other key element in Gandhi's strategy. Ahisma and satyagraha are based on the notion that the opponent and the protestor are one; thus, one approaches confrontation with deep compassion for the opponent. Gandhi teaches:

In satyagraha, it is never the numbers that count; it is always the quality, more so when the forces of violence are uppermost.

Then it is often forgotten that it is never the intention of a satyagrahi to embarrass the wrongdoer. The appeal is never to his fear; it is and must be, always to his heart. The satyagrahi's object is to convert, not to coerce, the wrongdoer. He should avoid artificiality in all his doings. He acts naturally and from inward conviction. (Cited in Easwaran 1978, 53)

Gandhi's struggle against the South African government and its leader, General Jan Smuts, lasted seven years but in the end was successful as the hated law, "the Black Act," was overturned. Gandhi and his followers were imprisoned, but through their steadfastness of purpose they won their case.

Gandhi returned to India in 1914. Gradually, he became involved in India's struggles against British domination. He also saw the connection between British control and India's treatment of its own people, particularly the untouchables. Gandhi called these people Harijans, or children of God, and called on Indians to end their cruel treatment of these people. Gandhi tell us, "All of us are one. When you inflict suffering on others you are bringing suffering on yourself. When you weaken others, you are weakening yourself, weakening the whole nation" (cited in Easwaran 1978, 56). Gandhi refused to go into temples where the Harijans were excluded. He said to the crowds, "There is no God here. If God were here, everyone would have access. He is in every one of us" (ibid., 59). As a result of Gandhi's campaign, many places that were once off-limits to the untouchables opened their doors.

Again, Gandhi taught from example. He travelled third class on the train and went to live with the Harijans and helped them improve their health and sanitation procedures. His followers did the same.

Gandhi drew many to the cause of non-violent resistance against the British. One of the most famous followers was Jawaharlal Nehru, who was from a wealthy Indian family. After meeting Gandhi, Nehru gave up his expensive lifestyle and put his energy and wealth into Gandhi's movement. Nehru's father, Motilal, was very upset by this and went to Gandhi pleading with him to give him his son back. In exchange, Motilal offered to give Gandhi money in support of the movement for independence. Gandhi replied, "Not only do I want your son, I want you, and your wife, and your daughters and the rest of your family too" (cited in Easwaran 1978, 65). The entire family did become members of Gandhi's movement, starting with Motilal himself. Gandhi, as a personal presence, had a powerful effect on people. His warmth and humour were infectious. Even British administrators were warned to stay away from Gandhi or they, too, would become converts to the movement.

Gandhi was a formidable opponent because his actions were so unpredictable. Eknath Easwaran (1978) states, "Every move he made was spontaneous; every year that passed found him more youthful, more radical, more experimental. No one knew what he was going to do next, for his actions were prompted not by stale calculations of what seemed politically expedient, but by a deep intuition" (65). These intuitions often came to Gandhi in meditation or sometimes in his dreams.

Gandhi's salt march is one of the best examples of spontaneous action. In 1930, the campaign for independence had reached a crucial point when the Indian Congress party raised the flag of freedom as a signal of a new era in the struggle for independence. India was very tense, waiting for either side to make a move. Gandhi was expected to provide leadership and he withdrew to his ashram to meditate. For weeks, he sat quietly while those around him urged him to act and, finally, the answer came to Gandhi in a dream. The British had passed a law according to which it became illegal for anyone in India to make his or her own salt. Gandhi saw that this was a perfect example of how the British exploited India, and he felt that the best way to confront the British was to march to the sea and to take some salt from the water there. This was the famous salt march.

Gandhi started with seventy-eight of his followers and walked twelve miles each day for twenty-four days. Gandhi was sixty-one years old at the time, yet he walked briskly and energetically for the entire length of the march. When Gandhi reached the water, a huge crowd was there to watch him as he took a small bit of salt from the sand. Immediately, huge crowds along the coastline gathered salt and then sold it in the cities. As a result, thousands of Indians were arrested and imprisoned, while many others were beaten and killed by the police. Throughout, however, the Indians maintained their peaceful protest. For a long period Gandhi remained free, but finally, the police came and arrested him at his ashram. When he went to prison, there were sixty thousand satyagrahri in jail. Gandhi, of course, was imprisoned several times during his life. He used his time there to pray, meditate, read, and answer his mail. Many people have seen the salt march as the defining moment in the move to eventual independence for India. Louis Fischer (1954), in his biography of Gandhi, states:

> The salt march and its aftermath did two things: it gave the Indians the conviction that they could lift the foreign yoke from their shoulders; it made the British aware that they were subjugating India. It was inevitable, after 1930, that India would some day refuse to be ruled, and more important, that England would some day refuse to rule.
>
> When the Indians allowed themselves to be beaten with batons and rifle butts and did not cringe, they showed that England was powerless and India invincible. The rest was merely a matter of time. (102)

Of course, independence did come to India after the Second World War, but not in the way Gandhi envisioned. India was divided into Hindu India and Muslim Pakistan, and in the process, thousands of people had to move and there was much violence. Gandhi fasted to help curtail the violence in Calcutta. Another burden he faced at the end of his life was the death of Kasturbai, in 1944. He deeply grieved her loss.

Gandhi was assassinated by a Hindu fanatic, who was upset at Gandhi's influence through his fast in Calcutta. When Gandhi was shot, his only words were "Rama," the Indian name for God.

Gandhi's main form of meditation throughout his life was mantra as he constantly repeated the word Rama over and over. Gandhi had been taught this mantra when he was young by a family servant, Rambha. The mantra was a constant source of strength for Gandhi throughout his struggles. Gandhi stated, "The mantram becomes one's staff of life and carries one through every ordeal. Each repetition has a new meaning, each repetition carries you nearer and nearer to God" (cited in Easwaran 1978, 65).

Gandhi found that the mantra of Rama made him joyful. As he walked or worked, he repeated it to himself. If Gandhi was involved in struggles that could produce anger and feelings of ill will, he found that the mantra settled his mind. As Easwaran (1978) comments, "Over the years, as the mantram penetrated below his deepest doubts and fears, he became established in joy" (118). Gandhi felt that you gradually become what you meditate on. If we meditate on God, then we become part of God. Meditation was a means for reuniting Gandhi with the source.

Besides the mantram, Gandhi meditated on the *Bhagavad Gita*. He particularly liked the second chapter. Gandhi felt that the verses of the second chapter were "inscribed" on his heart.

Gandhi was once asked to give a message to his people. He wrote on a small piece of paper, "my life is my message." For Gandhi, everything he did was a contemplative act. Easwaran (1978) says in his biography of Gandhi, "To those who met him, even many who came as enemies, he was the supreme artist who had made the smallest detail of his life a work of art" (125). Despite the fact that Gandhi had become a world figure whose activity affected the course of millions in India, he gave complete *attention* to every detail of his life. Through loving attention, he transformed himself, those around him, and eventually an entire nation. Easwaran has claimed, "Historians of the future, I believe, will look upon this century not as the atomic age, but as the age of Gandhi" (5). Gandhi is a powerful example of how contemplation can be applied to social action. His life and writings have inspired many, including Martin Luther King and Aung San Suu Kyi.

Black Elk

Black Elk was an Oglala Sioux and member of the Lakota tribe. The date of his birth is unclear although his daughter, Lucy, believed he was born in 1865 (Steltenkamp 2009). He died in 1950. His life spanned so many changes from being a young warrior, becoming a holy man and medicine man, a Catholic catechist, a father, and through the work of John Neihardt (2008) and Joseph Brown (1989), Black Elk has become known as one of the most famous Native Americans.

When Black Elk was around eight years old, he collapsed and was semi-conscious for twelve days. During this time he had a vision, which is recorded in *Black Elk Speaks* (Neihardt 2008). The vision is quite long and takes up twenty pages in Neihardt's book. Only elements of the entire vision can be included here. At the beginning of the vision, he saw forty-eight horses with swallows flying above them. The horses were in groups of twelve, with each group coming from one of the four directions (west, north, east, and south). Black Elk was taken to six grandfathers by the horses. The first grandfather gave him a cup of water, which symbolized that Black Elk would become a powerful healer; he also received bows and arrows to indicate that he would also be a warrior. Another grandfather represented *Wakan Tanka*. Wakan Tanka originally "referred to the totality of the spirit world, its incomprehensibility, and its mysterious, wondrous power. Over time, however, Lakota prayers that were in English simply came to invoke the Great Spirit" (Steltenkamp 2009, 11). The grandfather told Black Elk that "the fowls of the universe would help him" (26) At the end of the vision are the oft-quoted lines:

> Then I was standing on the highest mountain of them all, and round about beneath me was the whole hoop of the world. And while I stood there I saw more than I can tell and I understood more than I saw; for I was seeing in a sacred manner the shapes of all things in the spirit and the shape of all shapes as they must live together like one being. And I saw that the sacred hoop of my people was one of many hoops that made one circle, wide as daylight and as starlight, and in the center grew one mighty flowering tree to shelter all the children of one mother and one father. I saw that it was holy. (Neihardt 2008, 33)

The next few years were ones that contained the battle at Little Bighorn, where Custer's army was defeated by the Sioux. Black Elk was only ten years old at the time, but he witnessed the killing and the dead bodies. When Black Elk was sixteen, he had his first experience as medicine man and healer. With the help of Red Feather, Black Elk had his community re-enact aspects of his vision with some people riding on horses and others performing roles that Black Elk and Red Feather identified. Michael Steltenkamp (2009) writes that Black Elk reported that many of the sick were healed and that even the horses were better after the ritual had been performed (48). He had earned the role of medicine man.

Another important experience also occurred around this time. Black Elk had what is called *hanbleciya*, "the crying for a vision," also referred to as the vision quest. He was taken to a hill and left alone so he could connect with the spirit world. There he encountered an eagle, a chicken hawk, and a black swallow, and he started to cry for the relatives and friends who had died. During the experience, he also met two of his grandfathers. On returning to his tribe, the elders told Black Elk that he "was being called to greatness and encouraged him to use his gifts to help others" (Steltenkamp 2009, 51). Black Elk was now being asked not only to help his fellow Lakota but to reach out to all humanity.

Another role that Black Elk performed was that of *heyoka*. Sometimes translated as "clown," the heyoka "serves as a kind of Native therapist whose behavior provides a harmonizing element to the human condition, i.e. balances convention with its opposite" (Steltenkamp 2009, 88). Black Elk was known for his sense of humour. Once, when standing in front of his people giving a talk, he was wearing his wife's coat by mistake. After the talk, he joked with his wife that she should keep her clothes separate from his.

When Black Elk was around twenty years old, he joined Buffalo Bill's Wild West Show that toured England and Europe. One of the reasons for joining the show was that he wanted to see "the great world, and the ways of the white men" (DeMaille 1984, 245). This was Black Elk's first contact with Christianity, and he was favourably impressed when he saw people attending services in cathedrals.

Upon returning to his people, Black Elk found that there was great difficulty with crop failures, famine, and disease. His people began to express their anger, and tensions arose between the Sioux and the government. These tensions eventually led to the tragedy at Wounded Knee, in 1890, where Lakota were killed by US troops. Black Elk witnessed the disaster where many women and children were among the dead.

Two years after Wounded Knee, Black Elk married and eventually had three children – Never Showed Off, Good Voice Star, and Benjamin. During this period, more Lakota were converting to Christianity, and Black Elk converted to Catholicism. Kills Brave, who was a leader of a reservation town in South Dakota and a practising Catholic, convinced Black Elk to convert, which occurred in 1904. For many years, Black Elk was a catechist, and in this he was joined by many other Lakota including his lifelong friend, Kills Enemy. Black Elk would act as a missionary among his own people for many years. Steltenkamp (2009) suggests that his experience as a catechist was not unusual at the time and was also a continuation of his interest in Christianity, which had begun when he was in Europe. When he became a Catholic, he also took the name Nicholas Black Elk.

Black Elk's conversion and work as a catechist has created much discussion and controversy. Raymond J. DeMaille (2008), in an appendix to Neihardt's book, argues that both Black Elk's Native religion and Catholicism were important when he was interviewed by Neihardt for *Black Elk Speaks*:

> But when Neihardt reawakened in him the vivid reality of his visions and the realization that this white man had been led to him to learn about the Lakota path to the other world, the experience did not prompt him to reject the Catholic religion, but to reaffirm his traditional religion. Just as Black Elk regretted his action after the Wounded Knee Battle when he relied solely on his Ghost Dance vision and put aside the visions of his youth, he may have regretted putting aside Lakota belief and relying solely on Catholicism in middle age. None of the three were incompatible; all paths lead to the same transcendent truth. (315)

Joseph Epes Brown was another person who approached Black Elk towards the end of his life to inquire about Native rituals. Like the Neihardt experience, it was an opportunity for Black Elk to reaffirm his Native beliefs and practices. The result was Brown's book, *The Sacred Pipe: Black Elk's Account of the Seven Rites of the Oglala Sioux* (1989). According to Ake Hultkrantz, it became "the most widely read work on Plain Indians religion" (cited in Capps 1976, 91). Black Elk revealed the history and use of the pipe for prayer and ritual. The story behind the pipe was that it was given by White Buffalo Cow Woman. She came to the village of a man to whom she gave the pipe and told the people that the pipe would assure them "that Wakan Tanka would hear their prayers." She said, "With this sacred pipe you will walk upon the Earth; for the

Earth is your Grandmother and Mother and She is sacred. Every step that is taken upon Her should be as a prayer" (cited in Brown 1989, 6). In the traditional ritual, the stem of the pipe is pointed in the four directions (west, north, east, and south) and then towards the sky and the earth; finally, it is smoked:

> When offering the pipe, for example, one invokes the supernatural powers that reside above, below and in the cardinal directions. Tobacco grains accompany these offerings, and these grains represent all created things and all the intentions of the assembled. The pipe ritual thus includes all space, all creation and all the personal concerns brought by participants. Rising smoke represents the ascent of all this to Wakan Tanka. (Steltenkamp 2009, 168)

The other rites described in *The Sacred Pipe* include the keeping of the soul, *Inipi*; the rite of purification, *Hanblecheyapi*; crying for a vision, *Wiwanyag Wachipi*; the sun dance, *Hunkapi*; the making of relatives, *Ishan Ta Awi Cha Lowan*; preparing a girl for womanhood; and the throwing of the ball, *Tapa Wank Yap*.

Black Elk describes how the making of relatives, *Ishan Ta Awi Cha Lowan* creates peace in three ways:

> The first peace which is the most important, is that which comes within the souls of men when they realize their relationship, their oneness, with the universe and all its Powers, and when they realize that at the center of the universe dwells *Wakan-Tanka*, and that this center is really everywhere, it is within each of us. This is the real Peace, and the other are between two individuals, and the third is that which is made between two nations. But above all you should understand that there can never be peace between nations until there is first known that true peace, which as I have often said, is within the souls of men. (Cited in Brown 1989, 115)

This is a powerful spiritual vision that is universal in its appeal. Black Elk was able to convey that Wakan Tanka is in all creation and in ourselves. Realizing this, we can see the relatedness of things in a sacred manner.

Thomas Merton

Thomas Merton, a Catholic Trappist monk, made important connections between Christian and Buddhist forms of contemplation. He is certainly one of the most important contemplatives of the twentieth century.

Merton was born on 31 January 1915, in Paris. His mother, Ruth, was American, and he remembered her as a "slight, thin, sober little person with a serious and somewhat anxious face" (Merton 1948, 117). In Merton's view, his mother was rather "cerebral." His father, Owen, was from New Zealand, and he was an artist who painted landscapes with watercolours.

Merton's mother died from stomach cancer when he was six years old. Merton (1948) recalled, "A tremendous weight of sadness and depression settled on me. It was not the grief of a child, with pangs of sorrow and many tears. It had something of the heavy perplexity and gloom of adult grief, and was therefore all the more of a burden because it was, to that extent, unnatural" (20). His mother's death made Merton's childhood insecure, and he also held some bitter feelings about his mother. Later, in life, he stated, "perhaps solitaries are made by severe mothers" (cited in Furlong 1980, 15).

Merton spent most of his early childhood in the New York area. However, in 1924, his father moved back to France. Although Merton was upset by the move, his years in France were important. Rural France and the Catholic culture appealed to Merton, and he felt very much at home there although he was unhappy at school. Three years later, he and his father moved to England. After living a few years there, Merton suffered the loss of his father. Thus, as a young teenager, Merton found himself without his parents, and his godparents became his guardians.

Merton went to Oakham public school in England and did well, particularly in languages. Before going to university, at Cambridge, Merton had his first profound spiritual experience. He had a vision of his father that seemed very real and led to an immediate sense of inadequacy and a need for spiritual connection. Merton (1948) writes:

> And now I think for the first time in my whole life I really began to pray ... praying out of the very roots of my life and of my being and praying to the God I had never known, to reach down towards me out of His darkness. (114)

Merton studied one year at Cambridge, but it was a disaster. He did not do well in school and also fathered a child. Guilt not only arose from this event but also from the fact that he did not keep in touch with the child or the mother, who were both to die in an air raid in London during the Second World War.

Merton decided to move to the United States and study at Columbia University. At Columbia, he was strongly influenced by one of his professors, Mark Van Doren, who taught English there. Merton (1948) writes, "The influence of Mark's sober and sincere intellect, and his manner of dealing with his subject with perfect honesty and objectivity and without evasions was remotely preparing my mind to receive the good seed of scholastic philosophy" (141–2).

It was also at Columbia that Merton decided to become a Roman Catholic. Some of Merton's close friends at Columbia were spiritually oriented and supported Merton's own spiritual inclinations. Merton (1948) describes his decision:

> Suddenly, I could bear it no longer. I put down the book, and got into my raincoat, and started down the street. I crossed over, and walked along by the grey wooden fence, towards Broadway, in the light rain.
>
> And then everything inside me began to sing. I had nine blocks to walk. Then I turned the corner of the 121st Street and the brick church and presbytery were before me. (212–13)

He encountered the priest on the street and shortly thereafter declared his wish to become a Catholic.

His Columbia friends attended his First Communion. Although Merton still went to wild student parties and had affairs with girls, from the moment of his conversion he was a devoted Catholic. He went to Mass often, more than once a week, and regularly went to Confession and Communion. He also learned the rosary and did a lot of spiritual reading. But he still was confused. One of his close friends, Bob Lax, said to him while they were walking down Sixth Avenue in New York one day that the only important task in life was to be a saint and all you had to do was want it badly enough. He went to Mark Van Doren and asked if this was true, and Van Doren agreed that it was. Merton wondered why his non-Christian friends such as Lax, who was Jewish, could see things so clearly.

Merton finished his M.A. and began work on a novel. While living the life of a struggling writer, one day with friends, the thought entered his mind: "I am going to be a priest." He told his friends, and they thought it was another temporary enthusiasm. However, from this moment, Merton's life began to change as he gave up the wild parties, girls, and drinking. He went to a Franciscan monastery in New York to see if he could join, but they told him he had to wait because applicants were only accepted once a year. His application, however, was rejected when Merton told a Franciscan of his past. Merton was crushed by the rejection, but he did not give up his desire to go to a monastery.

In what he felt was the most important year of his life – 1941 – Merton went to a retreat at the Trappist Monastery, Gethsemani, in Kentucky. When he arrived there, he immediately felt at home and wondered, again, whether he might be able to become a monk. In a brief conversation with Mark Van Doren, Van Doren had asked whether he still wanted to be monk and encouraged him to go ahead with his idea of becoming a priest. Merton seized upon this encouragement and decided to go to Gethsemani again for a Christmas retreat. When he arrived there, he applied to be a postulant and was accepted.

The life at Gethsemani was hard. There was no heating or air conditioning, and the monks were expected to do a great deal of manual labour. Silence was the rule as the monks could only speak to their superiors. The monks used signs to communicate. The food was vegetarian, and according to Merton, it was not well cooked and tasteless. The monks rose at two in the morning and retired at seven in the evening, and during their waking hours the day was structured around work and prayer.

Merton found that the simple life at Gethsemani sharpened his awareness and brought him closer to God. In these beginning years as a monk, Merton equated contemplation with concentration. The ability to see with the concentrated eye was to make his writing more detailed and much richer in effect. Merton recalled the two years as a novice monk as a very happy period in his life. The monastery provided a home and structure, which he had missed for most of his life.

However, near the end of his initial training, about two years after his arrival at Gethsemani, Merton reached a state of collapse. Part of this was sheer physical exhaustion because of the difficult routine at Gethsemani, but some of it may also have been due to the fact that Merton's desire to write was not being met. He discussed this need with his superiors, and they decided to support his writing if it dealt with Trappist life. This approval eventually led to *The Seven Storey Mountain* (1948). This autobiography, which describes his spiritual path to Catholicism and Gethsemani, became a worldwide best seller. The original hardback sold 600,000 copies. The book made Merton famous, and he began to receive voluminous mail from around the world.

Merton wrote *The Seeds of Contemplation* in the late 1940s. Some consider this to be Merton's best description of the contemplative life. It is not a how-to book but describes Merton's approach within the Catholic monastic tradition. Merton's definition of contemplation, which was cited in the first chapter of this book, is found in the updated version of the book, *New Seeds of Contemplation* (1972). It is worth citing again:

Contemplation is the highest expression of man's intellectual and spiritual life. It is that life itself, fully awake, fully active, fully aware that it is alive. It is spiritual wonder. It is spontaneous awe at the sacredness of life, of being. It is gratitude for life, for awareness and of being. It is a vivid realization of the fact that life and being in us proceed from an invisible transcendent and infinitely abundant Source. (1)

Life at Gethsemani was a struggle for Merton. He often felt constrained by his superiors and the life in general. His occasional feelings of anger at his superiors reinforced a sense of guilt.

Merton became the person responsible for teaching at the monastery; first, as the master of scholastics and, then, as the master of novices. One former student recalls his impressions of Merton:

The first time I saw him he was bouncing down the cloister, making all the signs we weren't supposed to make, and which he bawled us out for making. We were all going into the church and he was going in the opposite direction which I suppose was a part of the joke. He never wanted you to take him too seriously ... Everybody loved him. Some of the monks might think some of his ideas were wild, but he was much loved. You couldn't look up to him as an elder except in his spiritual teaching and his direction. (Furlong 1980, 219)

Although he enjoyed teaching immensely, this was another activity that made Merton tired. His overwork and conflicts would lead to periodic sickness where he would have to retire to the infirmary. In 1950, while he was in the infirmary, he saw the importance of solitude. He explains, "Solitude is not found so much by looking outside the boundaries of your dwelling as by staying within. Solitude is not something you must hope for in the future. Rather it is a deepening of the present, and unless you look for it in the present you will never find it" (cited in Furlong 1980, 178).

Throughout his life, Merton saw the need for quiet and solitude, not only for himself but for others as well. He once wrote in the 1950s, "Provide people with places where they can go to be quiet – relax minds and hearts in the presence of God ... Reading rooms, hermitages. Retreat houses without a constant ballyhoo of noisy 'exercises'" (cited in Furlong 1980, 186). Merton's vision has become more of a reality as retreat centres of various kinds have arisen all over North America.

The search for solitude led to Merton's desire for privacy at Gethsemani. Merton's writing had attracted new monks to the order, and the monastery had become overcrowded. Merton dreamed of being a hermit. Around this time, one of his books, *The Sign of Jonas*, was not approved by the church for publication. Merton wanted to transfer to an Italian monastery where the monks were almost entirely alone, but his request was thwarted.

During the 1950s, Merton came to terms with himself. He did not care so much about being the "good" monk and became more comfortable with himself. By the late 1950s, he was reading widely in many areas. He also ventured into literature from Eastern religions. By the early 1960s, Merton had become intensely interested in the issues of the day such as civil rights and the threat of nuclear war. He was corresponding with people about these issues, and many people came to see him at Gethsemani. Merton was also allowed to go to New York to see the Zen master, D.T. Suzuki, who was interested in Merton's work.

The 1960s also saw one of Merton's dreams come true as he was able to have his own hermitage, or small house, separate from the monastery. The hermitage brought him closer to nature as he enjoyed watching his surroundings and feeling part of nature. He even had a record player, and he particularly enjoyed the music of Mozart. Many people when they met Merton were struck by his personal presence, for example, the Indonesian ambassador to Washington, Dr. Soedjatmoko said:

> If there is one impression that has stayed with me all along it is a memory of one of the very few people I have known in this world with an inner freedom which is almost total. It was, I felt, an inner freedom which was not negative, in terms of something else, but it was like the water that constantly flows out of a well. (Cited in Mott 1984, 535)

Soedjatmoko saw Merton as a "living example of the freedom and transformation of consciousness which meditation can give" (ibid.). Near the end of his life, Merton (1968) looked at contemplation in the following manner:

> Duty of the contemplative life – (Duty's the wrong word) – to provide an area, a space of liberty, of silence, in which possibilities are allowed to surface and new choices – beyond routine choice – become manifest. To create a new experience of time, not as stoppage, stillness, but as "temps vierge" – not a blank to be filled or an untouched space to be conquered and violated, but to enjoy its own potentialities and hopes – and its own presence to itself. One's *own* time. But not dominated by one's ego and its demands. Hence open to others – *compassionate* time. (68–9, emphasis added)

Near the end of his life, Merton wrote the following: "Our real journey in life is interior; it is a matter of growth, deepening, and of ever greater surrender to creative action of love and grace in our hearts" (cited in Mott 1984, 543).

Thomas Merton died unexpectedly while he was in Asia in 1968. Shortly before his death, he spoke to a group of people representing different faiths in Calcutta. The words are at the heart of Merton's (1975) view of contemplation:

> And the deepest level of communication is not communication, but communion. It is wordless. It is beyond words, and it is beyond speech, and it is beyond concept. Not that we discover a new unity. We discover an older unity. My dear brothers, we are already one. But we imagine that we are not. And what we have to recover is our original unity. What we have to be is what we are. (307)

Many people today find Merton an inspiring figure for their own practice. Particularly important, from my perspective, was how he was able to explore contemplative practices from other traditions (e.g., Buddhism) and then connect these to his own Christian tradition. As we move through the twenty-first century, this ability to connect contemplative traditions should become even more significant.

Aung San Suu Kyi

Aung San Suu Kyi is the leader of the democratic movement in Burma. She was held under house arrest in that country for almost fifteen of twenty-one years beginning in 1989 until her release in November 2010. During that time, she received numerous awards, including the Nobel Peace Prize, in 1991. During the long years of house arrest, meditation was central to her life. After arising at 4:30 in the morning, she would meditate for one hour every day. Suu Kyi (1997) believes all human beings have a "spiritual dimension which cannot be neglected" (85):

> Meditation has helped to strengthen me spiritually in order to follow the right path. Also for me, meditation is part of a way of life because what you do when you meditate is to learn to control your mind through developing awareness. The awareness carries into everyday life. For me, that's one of the most practical benefits of meditation – my sense of awareness has become heightened. I'm much less inclined to do things carelessly and unconsciously. (92)

Suu Kyi sees herself as a Buddhist working primarily in the Theravada tradition. Her teacher is the Buddhist monk, U Pandita, who teaches a practical form of *vipassana*, or insight meditation (see chapter 3). U Pandita sees meditation as contributing to peace in the world and encourages laypeople to meditate. For centuries, people in Burma did not meditate but hoped to receive spiritual merit by feeding the monks. However, U Pandita and his late teacher, Mahasi Sayadaw, believe that a mass lay-meditation movement could purify society. In his biography of Suu Kyi, Peter Popham (2012) argues that meditation determined her political path more than any other influence (296).

Aung San Suu Kyi was born in 1945, in Rangoon, the capital of Burma. Her father was Aung San, who led the Burmese independence movement against Britain. He was able to negotiate independence in 1947 but was assassinated that same year. Aung San is seen as the father of modern Burma and is revered throughout the country. Suu Kyi's mother, Khin Kyi, held the position of ambassador to India and Nepal in the early 1960s, and Suu Kyi lived in New Delhi where she went to Lady Shri Ram College and studied politics. She then moved to England and studied philosophy, politics, and economics (PPE) at St. Hugh's College at Oxford. One of her professors there, Mary Warnock, remembers that Suu Kyi was "unlike any undergraduate I had taught before or have taught since. She was highly intelligent and articulate, though quiet and enormously polite" (cited in Popham 2012, 194). Once, in a seminar on John Locke, Professor Warnock was taken aback when Suu Kyi asserted that she was her grandmother in a former life. Popham, in his biography of Suu Kyi, states that her mother had made her study PPE but she was bored with her studies at Oxford and would have preferred to study forestry or English.

After graduating, Suu Kyi lived in London with her guardians, Lord and Lady Gore-Booth. Lady Pat Gore-Booth considered Suu Kyi almost as a daughter. The Gore-Booths' children were twin boys, and one of their friends who came to visit was Michael Aris. Aris was immediately taken with Suu Kyi and gradually she, too, warmed to him. Aris was interested in Tibetan studies, and when they discussed marriage this was an important asset in convincing Suu Kyi's mother, who would have preferred she marry someone from Burma. While they were courting, they carried out a long distance relationship as Aris ended up being a tutor to the royal family in Bhutan. Suu Kyi moved to New York, and she worked at the United Nations where, at the time, the secretary general was U Thant. U Thant, a Burmese, is generally considered to be one of the greatest secretaries general in the history of the United Nations; he held this position from 1961 to 1971. Suu Kyi served on the support staff to the committee on budgetary questions. While in New York, she also volunteered at Bellevue Hospital where she helped with derelicts and incurable patients. Some Sundays, she spent at U Thant's home overlooking the Hudson River, where she met many different people from Burma. Aris came to visit her in New York in 1970 where they were engaged, and they were married in London in 1972. They exchanged many letters during the time they were apart. In one of them she writes, "I ask only one thing, that should my people need me, you would help me to do my duty to them" (Popham 2012, 219). Michael Aris never wavered in his support of Suu Kyi's commitment to Burma. Because of her house arrest, they spent many years apart, and Suu Kyi was not able to return to England when Aris became ill with cancer and died in 1999.

After their marriage, they moved to Bhutan where Aris continued his work, and since Bhutan had just joined the United Nations, Suu Kyi provided some advice about that organization. When Suu Kyi became pregnant, they moved back to England. Their first child, Alexander, was born there. They moved to Oxford, where Aris began work on his doctorate based on his six years of work and research in Bhutan. During these years in Oxford, Suu Kyi was, in Popham's view, "the helpmate, the north Oxford housewife" (2012, 234). Their second son, Kim, was born in 1977. Suu Kyi began writing during the Oxford years, and her work included children's books and a short biography of her father, Aung San.

During the years in England, she visited her mother in Burma regularly, often taking her children. In 1988, she went to take care of her mother who had had stroke. Burma was controlled by the military, and there were protests against the government in August of that year. There were mass demonstrations that were brutally suppressed. Moved by what was happening, Suu Kyi decided to give a speech – which was the beginning of her leadership of the Burmese people. Since she had never spoken in such a large public forum, people did not know what to expect. In a strong, clear voice, she called for a multiparty system of government. The Swedish journalist, Bertil Linter, wrote at that time, "Everyone was absolutely taken aback by that speech. Here was this tiny woman talking and everyone was spellbound. It was amazing. She looked like her father and she sounded like him too" (cited in Popham 2012, 55).

Suu Kyi helped found the National League for Democracy (NLD) but was put under house arrest in 1989. She was detained for fifteen of the next twenty-one years, until her most recent release in 2010. Before she was arrested, she was campaigning throughout Burma. During that campaign, an incident occurred that Popham calls the defining moment in her political life. Near the town of Danubyu, she and forty supporters were ordered not to walk in procession. They were walking on the side of the road while soldiers had their guns aimed at Suu Kyi. Defying the orders of the military, and risking her life, Suu Kyi decided then to walk in the middle of the road. She felt the orders were unreasonable. The soldiers' rifles were aimed at her but they did not shoot. Popham writes, "It was this incident, which, more than any other, created the mystique of Aung San Suu Kyi, while at the same time – in this land of the zero-sum game – effectively dismantling that of the army" (127). Some Burmese began to see her as a *bodhisattva*, or a holy person who devotes her life to relieving the suffering of others. Suu Kyi is not comfortable with attempts to deify her but it is also clear that spiritual and ethical concerns arising from her Buddhist beliefs are central to who she is.

Suu Kyi's political work is clearly in the tradition of Gandhian non-violence. Popham writes that for Suu Kyi "non-violence was a must" (116). He compares her to Gandhi in that she has the same quality of embodying the democratic hopes of her country as well as its "pride, its courage, its community-transcending solidarity, its will to shake off centuries of tyranny and reinvent itself" (371). Meditation has been central to Suu Kyi's political work. Popham makes the point that her practice of *metta*, or loving-kindness meditation as taught by U Pandita was crucial to her development as a leader. In metta, one sends thoughts of well-being to others, even one's opponents (see chapter 3). Before she started her practice, Suu Kyi was harshly critical of the head of the Burmese government, U Ne Win, and accused him of causing "the nation to suffer for 26 years." Popham writes, "If she had listened to U Pandita before making that speech, those harsh words against the tyrant might have gone unsaid" (296). Popham speculates that she might have avoided arrest at that time had she used more compassionate words.

Aung San Suu Kyi (1997) talks about the importance of compassion in her work:

> We put a great emphasis on *metta*. It is the same idea as in the biblical quotation: "Perfect love casts out fear." While I cannot claim to have discovered "perfect love," I think it's a fact that you are not frightened of people whom you do not hate. Of course, I did get angry occasionally with some of the things they did, but anger as passing emotion is quite different from the feeling of sustained hatred or hostility. (163)

Metta is also the founding principle of her party, the National League for Democracy. When asked about the founding principle, Suu Kyi said:

> It is metta. Rest assured that if we should lose this metta, the whole demo-
> cratic party would disintegrate. Metta is not only to be applied to those that
> are connected with you. It should be applied to those who are against you.
> Metta means sympathy for others. Not doing unto others what one does not
> want done to oneself ... So our league does not wish to harm anyone ... We
> are an organization that is free from grudge and puts metta to the fore.
> (Cited in Popham 2012, 312)

As this chapter is being written, in October 2012, Aung San Suu Kyi is touring the world and asking that the sanctions that have been imposed on Burma be ended since democratic reforms have begun. She is now an elected member of her legislature and head of the NLD. Suu Kyi has been criticized as "the perfect hostage" in that her stance of non-violence seemed to be leading nowhere (Wintler 2008). With recent events, however, Popham (2012) argues that not only has her non-violent stance changed Burma but also it has "changed the world" (388). Popham writes, "Suu changed Burma by throwing open the windows of her stale and stagnant homeland and letting the winds of the world blow in" (ibid.). Suu Kyi sees what is happening in Burma as a model to other countries in Asia in making them more democratic. Her work has had impact on Gene Sharp, who has written an important book on non-violence entitled, *From Dictatorship to Democracy: A Conceptual Framework for Liberation* (2012). This book has been translated into more than thirty languages and describes non-violent change that has occurred around the world. This book has inspired non-violent activists including the Serbian activist group called Otpor, whose non-violent protests led to the downfall of Milosevic in 2000. Sharp's book was first inspired by his visit to Burma and the impact of Suu Kyi's non-violent stance. He met with many people there, and in Sharp's words, Suu Kyi's "heroism and inspiration" were fundamental to his book, which continues to inspire non-violent movements around the world. This is the basis for Popham's claim that Aung San Suu Kyi has changed the world.

Summary

The eight contemplatives are different in many ways and represent various faith traditions. Their approaches to meditation also differ. The

Buddha focused on mindfulness and awareness, Emerson contemplated on his walks in nature, and Gandhi used the mantra "Ram." Merton used several forms of meditation from both his Catholic monastery training and from his interest in Buddhism. Dance and the arts were at the centre of Rumi's practice, while sacred rituals were Black Elk's primary practice. Metta, or loving-kindness, is central to Aung San Suu Kyi's meditation practice. However, we can also find in these contemplatives Merton's unity. It is clear each had a personal presence, and, yes, even a radiance that arose from his or her practice. This presence is evident in their warmth, humour, and joy. They represent examples of how contemplation can let us live life to the fullest. They were also human beings who cared deeply about those around them and who attempted to serve others by teaching or social action. They acted compassionately in the manner that Karen Armstrong (2006, 2011, 2012) has discussed.

It is my belief that we can call on them as well other teachers to whom we feel a connection. By calling on their presence, they can inspire and support our practice. At the same time, it is important that we remember the phrase, "if you meet the Buddha on the road, kill him." The contemplatives should not become figures whose teachings we accept without reservation. We need to test their teachings against our own experience and our own practice.

Chapter Five

The Invisible World

Crazy Horse dreamed and went into the world where there is nothing but the spirit of all things. That is the real world behind this one, and everything we see here is something like a shadow from that world.

Black Elk

For centuries, across cultures, people have sensed a vaster reality beyond the physical. Lao-Tzu called this dimension the "Tao," Plato referred to it as the "invisible world," Jung described it as the "collective unconscious," and David Bohm, the physicist, has named it the "implicate order.' Despite this long tradition, modern-day reality is rooted in materialism and gives little credence or possibility to the invisible world. Yet, now there are signs of awakening to the non-visible world. For example, there is growing interest in the cosmologies of Indigenous peoples, which almost always includes references to this world.

Why should we be interested in the non-visible world? First, creative people throughout the centuries have gathered inspiration from this world through the muse. The invisible world has been a primary source of creativity by both artists and scientists. Albert Einstein (1984) said, "The most beautiful experience we can have is the mysterious. It is the fundamental emotion which stands at the cradle of true art and true science" (40). Second, through various experiences such as near-death and heightened consciousness, the invisible world can be nourishing and even transforming. William James wrote that contact with the invisible world can "make new men." People who claim contact with the invisible world speak of being in the presence of a great harmonious energy that sustains them in their daily life. The research on the effects of near-death experience is one example of these data (Moody 1988; Long 2010). People who have practised meditation for many years can sense the non-visible world and feel that it nourishes their inner life. Finally, many people see the non-visible reality as part of the order of the universe. It makes sense to people of many different traditions that there is this non-visible world that is connected to the physical world. Emanuel Swedenborg, the Swedish mystic, believed that there is a correspondence between the physical and the spiritual world and that the former is somehow a mirror of the latter. Swedenborg's view is similar to Crazy Horse's and provides a picture of the universe of multilevelled realities.

Jerome Singer (1990) summarizes the influence of the non-visible world:

> It [the non-visible world] affects us profoundly through subliminal messages, feeling tones, unconscious impulses and reactions, hopes and dreams, fears and specters, and glimpses into the sometimes frightening, sometimes glorious realms of possibilities. The invisible world is also the one from which inspiration comes, in which new connections may be seen, and where we can sense the relatedness of all that appears to be separated and distinct in the visible world. (2)

In this chapter, I describe different conceptions of the non-visible world. I proceed chronologically with the descriptions and finish with the work of David Bohm, and the views of Indigenous peoples. I also discuss the work of Christopher Bache (2008), who has written about "learning fields" that can arise in classrooms and affect the learning and growth of students. Of course, there are differences in these conceptions, which reflect the social-cultural views of the individuals involved. For example, Plato's vision is dualistic while Taoism is rooted in a non-dualistic view. One of the problems is that these portrayals are attempting to describe what is indescribable; yet, I believe that it is important to attempt the description, since despite wide differences in time and place, we witness a strong desire among human beings to connect to the invisible world. It is also helpful to view these descriptions as broad metaphors for the invisible world and avoid literal descriptions and interpretations. These descriptions point to a reality rather than describe it.

The Tao

The Tao, also spelled Dao, is described in the book *Tao Te Ching* by Lao-tzu. We know little about Lao-tzu except that he lived in China from 551 to 479 BC and may have been an archivist in one of the small kingdoms there. Stephen Mitchell (1988) summarizes Lao-tzu's contribution: "Like an Iroquois woodsman, he left no traces. All he left us is his book: the classic manual on the art of living written in a style of gemlike lucidity, radiant with humor and grace and large-heartedness and deep wisdom: one of the wonders of the world" (vii).

Lao-tzu describes how each person can come in harmony with the Tao, or the Way. The Tao is the larger unnamable reality of which we are a part. It is described as:

> The Tao is nowhere to be found.
> Yet it nourishes and completes all things. (41)

Although we cannot see the Tao, Lao-tzu suggests it nourishes and sustains all things. The Tao is the primary source of everything. In most teachings regarding the invisible world the non-visible world is primary and the physical world, our day-to-day reality, can be entrapping. If we lose this sense of order, suffering arises. If we assign to the physical world the primary reality, we end up grasping and holding on to physical things. Unfortunately, the physical world is transitory and is subject to decay and our attempt to control it, or make it permanent, is futile. On the other hand, Tao or the invisible world is "Unchanging / Infinite. Eternally Present" (25).

Lao-tzu also writes, "It [the Tao] is always present within you" (6). This teaching is fundamental to all sacred traditions as the invisible world is not separate from us or outside us. As Jesus said "the Kingdom of God is within" so the Tao resides within us. Our journey or task is to allow that which is within us to manifest itself. Unfortunately, our ego fears the Tao and struggles to maintain a sense of separateness from it. Today, it seems modern civilization has lost touch with the Way. Lao-tzu's words are prophetic:

> When man interferes with the Tao,
> the sky becomes filthy,
> the earth becomes depleted,
> the equilibrium crumbles,
> creatures become extinct. (39)

Lao-tzu is very explicit about the principle that if we can be in harmony with the Tao then we will be "perfectly fulfilled" (7). Although we cannot see or hear the Tao, Lao-tzu teaches that "when you use it, it is inexhaustible" (35). We can't use it up; the Tao is an infinite source of energy.

Most of the *Tao te Ching* discusses how we can live more in harmony with the Tao. The guidelines offered apply to all areas of life including governing, social activity, and family life. By being in harmony with the Tao, we find that peace and fulfilment arise spontaneously in our lives.

Plato

At the end of Book Six in the *Republic*, Plato makes the distinction between the visible and the intelligible worlds. The latter is actually invisible. Each world requires its own set of habits. Antonio de Nicolás (1989) suggests:

> Plato's whole educational enterprise is concerned with developing quality in the performance of our inner acts. It is in relation to this quality of performance that he is able to sort out different worlds and the claims of the members of his community. These inner acts performed through education and training rely on their similarity to an original, invisible form. (43)

After Plato introduces the two worlds, he describes the famous Allegory of the Cave. In the cave, prisoners are chained and see only shadows of themselves on the walls of the cave. The prisoners believe that these shadows are real. One prisoner is compelled to free himself and he sees the fire, which is the source of the shadows on the wall. He also is forced to climb up the ascent and leaves the cave to go outside where he sees objects, which are much clearer and more distinct. He also sees that the sun is the source of light as the fire was in the cave. He remembers the fate of his fellow prisoners and returns to teach them about what he has seen and learned. However, they are not ready for this wisdom, and like Socrates, the prisoner-teacher is killed by his fellow prisoners.

It is possible to see the cave and its shadows as the visible world of ordinary existence. The chains of the prisoner represent the limitations of time-space, and perception in the cave is ordinary sense perception. The escape from the cave represents the spiritual and philosophical quest for wisdom. The objects outside the cave can be seen as representing Plato's "Ideas or Eternal Forms, whose reality and permanence transcend by far those of the physical world" (Capaldi, Kelly, and Navia 1981, 69). The sun is the "Idea of the Good," which represents ultimate reality for Plato, who calls it "the universal author of things beautiful and right, parent of light and the lord of light in this visible world and the immediate source of reason and truth in the intellectual" (ibid.). To come in contact with the sun is in some ways a mystical experience, which then must be translated into reason. For Plato, philosophy itself involves a strong spiritual element. Plato wrote a letter to his friend Dionysius (the king of Syracuse) about the problems of systematically representing his work. He avoided a systematic presentation of his thought because:

> There is no way of putting it in words like other studies. Acquaintance with it must come rather after a long period of attendance on instruction in the subject itself and of close companionship, when, suddenly like a blaze kindled by a leaping spark, it is generated in the soul and at once becomes self-sustaining. (60)

Returning to the two worlds, the visible is perceptible but transitory. On the other hand, the invisible world is intelligible and eternal, and physical reality mirrors the world of Forms or Ideas. In other words, the table in the real world corresponds to the Idea of the table. This is similar, again, to Swedenborg's notion of correspondence between physical and spiritual reality. One problem with Plato's invisible world is that it appears static. Unlike the Tao, which contains infinite possibilities, Plato's invisible world can appear fixed.

To come in contact with the invisible world, Plato suggests various contemplative practices. For example, in the *Phaedo* 67c–d and in 79c–81a, he talks about creating the "experience after death," or of achieving experience "through practicing death," by accustoming the soul to "withdraw from all contact with the body and concentrate itself on itself alone by itself."

Pierre Hadot (2002) makes the case that ancient philosophy was not just an intellectual exercise but was primarily a contemplative practice. He states that the Platonic dialogues were a form of spiritual practice, which demanded self-inquiry and self-transformation. Hadot also refers to Plato's meditation on death. This meditation allowed the practitioner to see beyond the shadows of the world and live with present awareness. Hadot says the meditation on death helped create "Platonic self-awareness" (193).

Thomas McEvilley (2002) is another scholar who explores the spiritual practices of Plato, and he compares them to the *Upanishads*. McEvilley argues that both Plato and the Upanishads describe knowing in a similar manner. He writes that "Patanjali refers to the 'knowledge' which yoga seeks as 'the light of higher consciousness.'" Plato, similarly, speaks of the mind being "flooded with light" and refers to wisdom as a "blaze kindled by a leaping spark" (192).

Plato developed these practices to connect with the invisible world.

Dante

In *The Divine Comedy*, Dante Alighieri draws an elaborate picture of the invisible world; it is depicted as a journey from hell to heaven. This journey can be seen as a journey within ourselves where we finally awaken to a deeper wholeness and connectedness with the invisible world. In Dante's vision, there is no separation between our inner life and the invisible world.

Dante's journey starts in hell. Fortunately, Dante has been sent a guide, the poet Virgil, by his beloved Beatrice. Virgil represents reason that wisely guides Dante through hell and purgatory. Hell is a place where love is absent, and the individuals there are caught deeply in self-deception. Honesty is essential to spiritual growth, and Dante has placed those who are dishonest in the lowest pit in the Inferno. In an age where we constantly question the credibility of our leaders, Dante's vision is a painful reminder of the spiritual morass of our age.

In purgatory, individuals experience for the first time a sense of personal responsibility. People in purgatory have an urgent sense of time. Here people learn that growth and wholeness arise from attention. Helen Luke (1989) comments:

> The souls are unwilling to waste one moment of the daylight in spite of their great pleasure in talking to Dante. It is a point which awakens us to a truth so easily forgotten in this age – the truth that the way of individuation demands *attention*, not just for a few hours or weeks, or a few minutes a day, but ultimately, during every moment of our lives ... The experience of immortality will spring ultimately from constant attention to the "minute particular," in Blake's phrase. The point lies not in *what* we do, as the Puritans mistakenly defined this truth, but in the degree of our conscious awareness of every act and every impulse in their contexts outer and inner. True spontaneity is born of this awareness alone. (52–3)

Contemplation is a constant theme throughout *The Divine Comedy*. It is attention that we bring to each daily act that allows for a gradual sense of connectedness to evolve within ourselves and to the invisible world. In purgatory, humans begin to be attentive and present. Near the end of Dante's journey in purgatory, Virgil leaves Dante so that Beatrice may guide him through Paradise. In Paradise, Dante comes in contact with the joy and bliss of the invisible world. For 33 cantos Dante describes his vision of heaven. This is in inner heaven, as well as a depiction of the invisible world. Like the Tao, Dante's invisible world is a sustaining source, and is called the "bread of angels." Dante finds this bread through self-acceptance.

Near the end of his journey, Dante fully accepts himself and forgives himself and does this with joy. Joy and heaven are often linked, but Dante has made the connection through complete self-acceptance and forgiveness. As we immerse ourselves more deeply in the invisible realm, we feel more deeply both compassion and bliss.

Dante's journey through paradise involves travel to the planets. The last and highest of the planets that Dante visits is Saturn where the souls of contemplatives reside. As noted earlier, attention and contemplation are fundamental to Dante's vision. Through the contemplation, the individual soul immerses itself more fully in the invisible world. Beatrice, his guide in Paradise, says to him that it is through witnessing, seeing, and contemplating that we gain the ability to experience true bliss. Beatrice earlier states that light from God surrounds her and connects with her own sight and being. This light is similar to Plato's prisoner's view of the sun as the primary source of light and understanding. Both Dante and Plato also acknowledge that we can only access this source through some form of contemplation – reason or analysis will simply not be enough.

At the end of *The Divine Comedy*, Dante comes to his final vision. The last line refers to "the Love that moves the sun and the other stars" (Canto 33, 140–5). Like Rumi, Dante fully grasps that love is the animating principle of the universe. Dante saw the invisible world as Conscious Love that expresses itself through the form of the physical world (e.g., the sun and the other stars).

Swedenborg

Emanuel Swedenborg (1688–1772) was the Swedish scientist-mystic who at mid-life had a spiritual vision. His work has since influenced a variety of fields such as religion, philosophy, homeopathy, architecture, poetry, and art. The impact of his work is best seen in the book *Emanuel Swedenborg: A Continuing Vision*, edited by Robin Larsen et al. (1988).

Central to this vision is the concept of correspondence. For Swedenborg, the divine works most directly through the spiritual realm (the invisible world) and also through the physical world (the visible), although its appearance is dimmed as the material world becomes denser. Like Plato, Swedenborg sees objects and events in the physical world as the result of images and ideas in the spiritual world. Larsen et al. (1988) state:

> Swedenborg's original notion of correspondences, later more fully developed as a theory in his theological period, holds that nature is the symbolic manifestation of spirit or psyche. The world as we experience it is but a shadow of inconceivable spiritual realities, which it nonetheless prefigures in its intricacies and vital creativity.
>
> The realities hover next to each other, an existential hair's breadth apart, what he calls a "discrete degree." (492)

William Blake, the English poet-artist, was deeply influenced by Swedenborg and poetically encapsulates the idea of correspondence in the following lines:

> To see the world in a grain of sand,
> And heaven in a wildflower;
> Hold infinity in the palm of your hand,
> And eternity in an hour. (Cited in Larsen et al. 1988, 492)

Swedenborg saw the physical reality as a microcosm of a much vaster spiritual reality (the macrocosm). Michael Talbot (1991) has also made the connection between Swedenborg's thought and Bohm's holographic paradigm. Bohm's theory will be discussed later in this chapter, but Bohm suggests that the physical world, or what he calls the "explicate order," is connected to a deeper reality – the implicate order – which is an unbroken whole. Swedenborg also saw the spiritual reality (Bohm's implicate order) as indivisible. For Swedenborg (1905–10), everything is connected: "Nothing unconnected ever occurs, and anything unconnected would instantly perish" (2556).

For Swedenborg, like Dante, the ultimate reality is love (Hite 1988). Lewis Hite concludes:

> Love exhibits the character of an infinity of infinities. Among such infinities are the animal and plant series; also such series as the rational and moral

life. It is as member of such series and as constituting such series, that the individual is a proper function of the universe, and is related to the universe as a whole. (415)

As we immerse ourselves in the invisible world, we can experience love. Love is an ultimate form of connectedness where all separateness is viewed as illusion.

Swedenborg's description of spiritual reality can be found in his book, *Heaven and Hell*. His vision parallels other portrayals of the invisible world and has provided the inspiration for many, most notably, Helen Keller (2000).

Emerson

Swedenborg was one of the many thinkers who influenced the American transcendentalist Ralph Waldo Emerson. Although influenced by many thinkers, Ralph Waldo Emerson (2003) developed his own unique vision. He called the invisible the Over-Soul. The Over-Soul is:

that great nature in which we rest as the earth lies in the soft arms of the atmosphere; that Unity, that Over-Soul, within which every man's particular being is contained and made one with all other; that common heart of which all sincere conversation is the worship, to which all right action is submission; that overpowering reality which confutes our tricks and talents, and constrains every one to pass for what he is and to speak from his character and not from his tongue, and which evermore tends to pass into our thought and hand and become wisdom and virtue and power and beauty. (294–5)

The Over-Soul, like the Tao, is a source of "wisdom and virtue and power and beauty." Emerson sees the line between the physical and spiritual as a very thin one. He says the Over-Soul is "undefinable, unmeasurable; but we know that it pervades and contains us. We know that all spiritual being is in man ... there is no screen or ceiling between our heads and the infinite heavens, so is there no bar or wall in the soul, where man, the effect ceases and God, the cause, begins" (296). Emerson suggests that we can come in contact with the invisible through contemplation, which "redeems us in a degree from the conditions of time" (ibid.). If we can simply let the Over-Soul act through us, then we know the right thing to do. Emerson closes his essay on the Over-Soul with a vision similar to the Swedenborg/Blake vision:

Thus revering the soul, and learning, as the ancient said, that "its beauty is immense," man will come to see that the world is the perennial miracle which the soul worketh, and be less astonished at particular wonders; he will learn that here is no profane history; that all history is sacred; that the universe is represented in an atom in a moment of time; he will weave with a divine unity. He will cease from what is base and frivolous in his life and be content with all places and with any service he can render. He will calmly front the morrow in the negligency of that trust which carries God with it and so hath already the whole future in the bottom of the heart. (311)

By coming in contact with the invisible world, we answer wholeheartedly in the affirmative Einstein's fundamental question: Is the universe friendly?

William James

The American psychologist William James wrote about the invisible world in *The Varieties of Religious Experience* (2002). Robert Richardson (2007), in his biography of James, writes that *The Varieties of Religious Experience* is a "book so pervasive in religious studies that one hears occasional mutterings in the schools about King James – and they don't mean the Bible" (6). James focuses on the spiritual experiences that individuals had, which often included connections with the invisible world that he simply calls something "more." *The Unseen Universe, or Physical Speculations on a Future State*, written by Peter Guthrie Tait and Balfour Stewart (1875), influenced James as they wrote that the visible world may only be a small part of the cosmos. James (2002) holds that "many performances of genius" have their origin in the invisible world (556), and proposes "that whatever it may be on its *farther* side, the 'more' with which in religious experience we feel ourselves connected is on its *hither* side the subconscious continuation of our conscious life" (556–7, original emphasis). He uses the term "transmarginal consciousness" to describe the state of knowing about the invisible world (557). Like many others who describe the invisible world, James talks about it as a more "intimate" reality than the visible world:

Name it mystical region, or the supernatural region, whichever you choose. So far as our ideal impulses originate in this region (and most of them do originate in it, for we find them possessing us in a way for which we cannot articulately account), we belong to it in a more intimate sense than that in which we belong to the visible world, for we belong in the most intimate sense wherever our ideals belong. Yet the unseen region in question is not merely ideal, for it produces effects in this world. When we commune with it, work is actually done upon our finite personality, *for we are turned into new men*, and consequences in the way of conduct follow in the natural world upon our regenerative change. But that which produces effects within another reality must be termed a reality itself, so I feel as if we had no philosophic excuse for calling the unseen or mystical world unreal. (560, emphasis added)

The Varieties of Religious Experience had a profound impact on Bill Wilson, who founded Alcoholics Anonymous. Wilson wrote to Carl Jung and compared the transformation that occurs to a person in AA to the conversion experience described in James' book. We might say that this conversion is spiritual in nature since it occurs without a priest or religious authority figure but simply through talking to other alcoholics. I will write about Bill Wilson and AA at the end of this chapter and explore how the invisible world actually affects human behaviour.

James also refers to a "sense of Presence" (2002, 301) that is part of the invisible world. He cites a passage from Thoreau's *Walden* to give an example of this Presence:

But, in the midst of a gentle rain, while these thoughts prevailed, I was suddenly sensible of such sweet and beneficent society in Nature, in the very pattern of the drops, and in every sight and sound around my house, an infinite and unaccountable friendliness all at once, like an atmosphere, sustaining me, ... Every little pine-needle expanded and swelled with sympathy and befriended me. I was so distinctly made aware of the presence of something kindred to me, that I thought no place could ever be strange to me again. (Thoreau 1983, 177)

Being in touch with this Presence is part of the process of making new men and women that James refers to in the conversion experience. Bill W. had such an experience, which was central to the development of Alcoholics Anonymous.

Jung

Carl Jung, the Swiss psychologist, at the end of *Memories, Dreams, Reflections* (1981) wrote, "The decisive question for man is, is he related to something infinite or not? That is the telling question of his life. Only if we know that the thing that truly matters is the infinite can we avoid fixing our attention upon futilities and upon all kinds of goals which are not of real importance ... In the final analysis we count for something only because of the essential we embody, and if we not embody that, life is wasted" (325).

Jung's conception of the infinite lay in his notion of the collective unconscious. Collective unconscious is to culture what personal unconsciousness is to personal ego. It is the vast, yes, infinite realm of possibility. Jerome Singer (1990) comments on the collective unconscious:

> On the far side [of the collective unconscious] is the unknowable – that is, unknowable by any rational means. If it can be known at all, it has to be through a process of subjective knowing. That means that it comes to one person at a time, in a way unique to that person, and that it cannot be validated by any of the methods that are culturally approved in the rational, visible world. (43)

One way that we can access the collective unconscious is through archetypes. Archetypes are symbols that represent universal, or culturally specific themes. Often the archetype is an image that becomes predominant in one's life. For example, the Hero archetype encourages the adolescent to move away from the Great Mother archetype (Feinstein and Krippner 1988). Different archetypes can follow one another as various themes emerge in one's life. Symbols from nature such as the sun and water are universal archetypes. The archetypes can be compared to Plato's Ideas, or Forms, in that they exist in the invisible world and are manifested in various ways in the physical world.

Archetypes can be accessed as vehicles for personal integration. In psychosynthesis, there are various guided imagery activities that use symbols such as the rose to facilitate wholeness and connectedness. Sometimes, spontaneous images can emerge in meditation or daily life that can deepen one's connection to the invisible world. Jung saw these images as arising from the collective unconsciousness, and as extremely important to the individuation of the person.

Singer (1990) also draws the comparison of Jung's collective unconscious to Bohm's implicate order: "For Jung the collective unconscious was the fundamental reality, with human consciousness deriving from it. In a similar way, Bohm sees the implicate order as the fundamental reality with the explicate order and all its manifestations as derivative" (63).

Bohm

David Bohm (1980) was a physicist who developed a theory that the universe is like a hologram. A hologram is a three-dimensional image produced when a single laser light is split into two different beams. One beam is reflected off an object while the second beam collides with the reflected beam to form an interference pattern that is recorded on the film. What is particularly interesting about the pattern on the film is that any piece of the film will contain the image of the object. Holography, then, reflects the principle that has been outlined by Swedenborg that the microcosm reflects the macrocosm.

Bohm argues that the hologram can explain some of the unusual behaviour seen in subatomic physics. Physicists refer to the behaviour of some subatomic particles as non-local, that is, they don't behave according to the normal laws of time and space. For example, two particles that seem unconnected and are not physically close to one another seem to move in common patterns. Bohm explains this behaviour through his concept of enfolded (implicate) and unfolded (explicate) orders. The implicate order is the non-visible world that lies behind the explicate order in an interconnected whole.

The example of implicate and explicate orders is found in Bohm's example of a jar full of glycerin where a drop of ink is placed in the jar. If we stir, the ink disappears (i.e., it becomes enfolded). However, if we stir in the opposite direction, the ink will appear (i.e., it becomes unfolded). The whole, however, is not static. Bohm has introduced the concept of *holomovement* in an attempt to portray the dynamism of the universe. Each particular object or event that we see as separate is actually part of this holomovement. Although we see each object and event as separate, these events and objects are part of a whole.

Bohm's work has also been connected with the research of Karl Pibram, who argues that the brain is like a hologram. Taken together, Michael Talbot (1991) says, "Our brains mathematically construct objective reality by interpreting frequencies that are ultimately projections from another dimension, a deeper order of existence that is beyond both space and time: The brain is a hologram enfolded in a holographic universe" (54).

Bohm and Weber (1982) speculated that this implicate order is like the invisible world of the mystic. In an interview, Bohm stated that the implicate order "could equally well be called Idealism, Spirit, Consciousness ... The separation of the two – matter and spirit – is an abstraction. The ground is always one" (40). Like Dante, Bohm also explored the importance of contemplation and attention in coming in contact with the invisible world: "At the present, our whole thought process is telling us that we have to keep our attention here ... Contact with eternity is in the present moment, but it is mediated by thought. It is a matter of attention" (cited in Talbot 1991, 261).

The way to the invisible world, as explained by Dante and Bohm, is through careful attention to the here and now. Through conscious attention, we are no longer bounded by ego chatter and belief systems; instead, the universe and the invisible world can be revealed to us.

Indigenous Wisdom

Michael Talbot (1991) makes the connection between Bohm's holographic reality and the shamanistic thinking of Indigenous peoples. Indigenous peoples see reality as deeply interconnected. The Hawaiian Kahunas, for example, see everything as connected, and the shaman sees himself in the centre of this interconnected web. Within the web, every point is a centre. Talbot comments, "Like Bohm, who says that consciousness always has its source in the implicate, the aborigines believe that the true source of the mind is in the transcendent reality of dreamtime" (289). Dreamtime is another metaphor for the implicate order and is the primary reality that Crazy Horse refers to in the quote at the beginning of this chapter.

Douglas Sharon (1978) suggests that implicate/explicate order can be found in most Indigenous traditions: "Probably the central concept of shamanism, wherever in the world it is found, is the notion that underlying all the visible forms in the world, animate and inanimate, there exists a vital essence from which they emerge and by which they are nurtured. Ultimately everything returns to this ineffable, mysterious impersonal unknown" (49).

This is why the shaman takes the drug so that he or she can come more directly in contact with the dream world. The journey into the spirit realm is like a pilgrimage. The main reason for embarking on this pilgrimage is that the shaman is concerned about maintaining the balance between the physical world and the spirit world.

Sometimes, the pilgrimage is actually a physical journey. For example, the Huichol Indians, who live in the Sierra Madre Occidental of central Mexico, make a sacred journey to Wirikuta, hundreds of miles from their own community. The Huichol Indians take this journey so that they can retrace the steps of their ancestors and in doing so actually come in contact with the realm that the ancestors inhabit. In taking this journey,

Maybury-Lewis (1992) claims that the "Huichols take this journey so that they can 'find their lives' after the manner of the Ancient Ones" (224). The shaman gives them the drug peyote to enter into the spirit world. Some of the Huichols find this experience so powerful that they want to stay in paradise, which would mean death on the physical plane. The shaman must guide them so that they can return and bring their vision of the spirit world into daily life. Through this experience, the Huichols realize that the transitory existence on the physical plane is made whole by the mystical experience. According to David Maybury-Lewis, "It is this knowledge that gives meaning to their lives and accounts for their insistence that the Huichol way of life is the most beautiful on earth" (228).

Maybury-Lewis contrasts the experience of Aboriginal connection to the invisible world with our secular world:

> We live in a world that prides itself on its modernity, yet is hungry for meaning. At the same time it is a world that marginalizes those very impulses that fill the void. The pilgrimage toward the divine, the openness to knowledge that transcends ordinary experience, the very idea of feeling at one with the universe, these are impulses which we tolerate at the fringes, where they are held at bay by our indifference. (231)
>
> Shorn of the knowledge that we are part of something greater than ourselves, we lose also the sense of responsibility that comes with it. It is this connectedness that tribal societies cherish and that we cannot bring ourselves to seek. But if we do not listen to other traditions, do not even listen to our inner selves, then what will the future hold for our stunted and over-confident civilization? (234)

In the previous chapter, the visionary experiences of Black Elk were described and the practices that he used to access the invisible world. One of the practices is the "crying for the vision," or the vision quest. Through fasting and exposing oneself to nature there is an opportunity to connect with the invisible world through dreams or images.

Making New Men and Women

William James argued that the invisible world can have a positive effect on human behaviour from the "performance of genius" to making "new men." I would like to describe two examples of how this claim can be supported.

Alcoholics Anonymous

Bill Wilson, who founded Alcoholics Anonymous, had experiences of the invisible world, which were instrumental in the development of AA. At one of the low points in his life, Bill W., as he was commonly known, had a mystical experience that was instrumental in turning his life around. Robert Thomsen (1975) describes this moment in his biography of Bill W.:

> In that very instant he was aware first of a light, a great white light that filled the room, then he suddenly seemed caught up in a kind of joy, an ecstasy such as he would never find words to describe. It was as though he was standing high on a mountaintop and a strong clear wind blew against him, around him, and through him – but it seemed a wind not of air but of spirit – and as this happened he had the feeling that he was stepping into another world, a new world of consciousness, and everywhere there was a wondrous feeling of Presence which all his life he had been seeking. Nowhere had he ever felt so complete, so satisfied, so embraced. (201)

The moment passed, but it was the beginning of Bill's path towards recovery and starting AA. Central to AA are the twelve steps that form the path to overcoming addiction.

One of the twelve steps is a belief in a higher "Power greater than ourselves that can restore our sanity" (Thomsen 1975, 333). He also felt there was a "mysterious ingredient" in the concept of anonymity that held AA together. At the core, it was the experience of one drunk simply talking to another drunk, and for Bill, when this happened he felt "himself drawing closer to some indefinable force. Then he was truly living in the now ... Conscious simply of the person he was with, he would become aware only of the moment, the immensity and movement of the moment. Sometimes when this happened it was almost as if distant chords of music had begun to sound, but he could never say what struck them" (298).

Bill W. recognized that it was difficult to talk about the experience of the invisible world. Yet, the power of the twelve-step method has spread around the world in all kinds of groups that gather to deal with various forms of addiction. Alcoholics Anonymous has been referred to as the "most significant phenomenon in the history of ideas in the twentieth century" (Kurtz and Ketchum 1992, 4). AA and all these other groups have helped develop new men and women that William James felt could arise from contact with the invisible world.

The Living Classroom

Christopher Bache (2008) has written about how the invisible world is present in teaching. Over the years of teaching at the post secondary level, he was witnessed "learning fields" grow around the courses he teaches. He argues that a group mind develops that can affect subsequent classes. Bache teaches courses in religion at Youngstown State University in Ohio, and he has practised meditation himself for many years. He cites research to support his claim of fields, including the work of Dean Radin (2006). He suggests that a "learning field reflects and embodies the cumulative learning of all the students through the years who have ever taken a specific course with a specific professor" (Bache 2008, 53). Bache makes the distinction between a learning field in a course, that is, course field, which develops over time, and the class field, which is the current group he is teaching: "When the course is under way, the energy that these students will encounter will be not just their professor's energy and not just the collective energy of the students present in the room but also the energetic residue of the learning of all the students who have taken this course before them" (55).

One student described her experience of the learning field:

> All of us who have been in your classes felt a deep connection to one another. We don't know what it is. We only know that it is there. All that I know is that I have felt something binding us all together ... Imagine all of this taking place on a college campus. A college class that wasn't only a class it was community, semester after semester. (44)

This collective energy resides below conscious awareness but can impact learning in the classroom. One student described her experience of the learning field like this:

> Instead of hearing your lectures with my Brain-Mind-Intellect, I actually heard you from somewhere else ... Heart-Soul maybe? Ears of a type that I hadn't been exercising. They had atrophied. You gave them a workout. Or the class field was so intense that it penetrated my controlling dominant brain-mind and vibrated my heart-soul like cardiac shock paddles to bring it to life.
>
> The result? I'm becoming who I was *long* ago. The field by-passed my intellect and went directly to my heart to pry it open ... I now know what I

had deeply buried in me for years, and the gift of folks in the classroom. It didn't come from me alone. (28)

The result of using a learning field is what Bache calls *great learning*. Great learning is transformative and can reveal itself in many ways including "when students write essays that surprise even themselves" (63).

I have taught a course in Holistic Curriculum since 1985, and in 1988 I introduced meditation as a requirement (see chapter 7) and have experienced what Bache has written about. In the summer of 2012, many of the papers of my students in my Holistic Curriculum were so good that I felt they could be put together in a book. One student, Maria Karmiais, who teaches children with special needs at the elementary level, wrote about her experience working with three boys who faced different challenges in her classroom. One part of this paper is worth quoting at length as it conveys young people's capacity for compassion:

> Sometimes keeping love present in a classroom space means ignoring the black print on the page and leaving lots of room for white space. Part of the transformative nature of keeping love present that Miller describes in his work is fostering compassion in the classroom (2010). Compassion manifests itself in different ways and I have more often than not felt like my students were in fact being my biggest teachers in this regard. A few years ago when I taught Grade 3, I had three boys in my class each with a physical disability. Abid had Duchene's Muscular Dystrophy. Rohan had suffered a rare stroke as an infant that left him partially paralyzed on the right side of his body. James was hard of hearing and was joining the regular classroom setting for a small class placement in a school for the deaf. By the description of these three boys you might think that I was teaching a special needs class but, in fact, these boys were part of the group of the twenty-three students I had that year in a regular classroom setting. My biggest concern was that the other children might exclude or tease these boys because their differences were physically evident. My worst fears never came to pass and as far as I could see or know my three boys with special needs were treated with kindness and respect. What I didn't expect and could not have anticipated was how knowing these three children would help to transform my view of children with special needs.
>
> Having these three boys in my class was another reminder to look beyond the surface. What I discovered that year is that each of these boys had a rich inner life of which I had the opportunity to merely glimpse. Each of these

boys was surrounded by loving families. James' mom ensured that he was engaged in a variety of opportunities to explore the world outside of school. James himself was an incredibly bright boy who was determined to do and be his best. All three boys developed a close friendship with each other and with one of their classmates, Abdul. Abdul demonstrated more patience and kindness with his friends at the age of eight than I have seen from many an adult. Of the three, James was most eager to demonstrate how much in common he had with his peers. He was determined to be seen as an equal. For me he was exceptional not because his ministry label identified him as such but because of the common humanity he shared with his classmates and indeed all beings.

Abid's story that year was not one of trying to fit in but of really fighting for his life. After the winter holiday break, Abid returned to school for one morning only to go home sick. Within the week he was diagnosed with a brain tumour and had surgery to remove it. Other than Rohan, whose family visited Abid in hospital, none of the other children saw him again as he did not return to school that year. My children made cards for him and we made a book to share with him. The teachers of our school got together to knit him a blanket. Every time I went to the hospital to visit Abid, I brought something with me from someone at school. I visited Abid many times after his surgery. First I visited him, at Sick Kids hospital and then at Bloorview Rehab hospital. One of his parents was always by his side. It would be a long, difficult road for recovery for Abid. The most frustrating part for him was being unable to talk for a full six months after the surgery. I sensed his frustration and really his anger when he would attempt to talk during my visits and all that would come out of his mouth were inaudible wailing sounds. How do you console a child with ideas and a voice who has lost his ability to speak? His mother would try to soothe him and I too attempted to remind him to be patient but, it all seemed so hollow. Just like I had experienced in other moments of my career, I was in a place beyond words. There was really nothing I could do or say. All I could do was be present.

A year later, Abid was out of the hospital but he was attending a different school. Abid was now permanently confined to a wheelchair and he needed to go to a school that could accommodate his new needs. I went to visit him there during a lunch hour with Rohan, James, and the SNA (Special Needs Assistant) that supported these boys when they were in my classroom. Abid was talking again and happy to tell us about his new school, his new classmates and his teachers. When it was time to leave, Rohan kneeled in front of Abid's wheelchair and spoke to Abid's legs. He said: "I hope you feel better soon so that you can walk again." Abid looked at his friend and said quietly and gently: "My legs aren't going to get better, this is how I am now." Sometimes as a teacher you are able to bear witness to such profound moments of compassionate love between others that you cannot help to feel anything but blessed.

Rohan was a student that I had the pleasure to teach for two years. I taught him in Grade 3 and then again when he was in Grade 5, I was assigned to teach the HSP (Home School Program) class. The HSP class is intended to provide support in math and language for half of the instructional day for students who are functioning two or more years below grade level. Rohan's SNA would often refer to him as a little Buddha because nothing ever seemed to trouble or upset him. I never saw him angry. He never held a grudge. He never complained. He was kind, patient and persevered. He even demonstrated persistence in gym class and did his best to complete every task despite his physical limitations. Upon his graduation from our elementary school, I had the honour of giving him one of our school awards. Seeing him walk onto the stage to receive his award was one of the proudest moments of my career. His eyes were beaming and his smile was full of joy. I felt like I was the one who received the award!

I asked Maria if I could share her paper with others; I gave it to my wife and she was very moved when she read the passage above. This was not the only outstanding paper in my class. There were many others that I believed represented "great learning." I believe the learning field in my course has become more powerful over the years.

The living classroom is supported by the invisible world and leads to learning that goes beyond the acquisition of knowledge and is truly transformative.

Summary

Our journey through various conceptions of the vision of the invisible world has revealed certain principles regarding its importance, such as the following:

1 The invisible world and visible worlds are interconnected. It is possible to see physical reality as a microcosm of the larger invisible world (the macrocosm) as depicted in the holographic view of reality as described by David Bohm.

2 Dante, Rumi, Gandhi, and others believed that at the core of the invisible world is love. Gandhi (1999) wrote:

Scientists tell us that without the presence of the cohesive force among atoms that comprise the globe of ours, it would crumble to pieces and we would cease to exist; and as there is a cohesive force in blind matter so must there be in all things animate, and the name for that cohesive force among animate beings is love.

True love is boundless like the ocean and, swelling within one, spreads itself out and, crossing all boundaries and frontiers, envelops the whole world.

It is my firm belief that it is love that sustains the earth. There only is life where there is love.

The law of love, call it attraction, affinity, cohesion if you like, governs the world. (55–7)

3 The invisible world can nourish and sustains us. In Emerson's words, it is the fount of "wisdom, virtue, power and beauty." Scientists and artists have claimed that it is a source of inspiration. As William James and researchers on the near-death experience (Long, 2010) have noted, contact with the invisible world can lead to personal growth and transformation.

4 The invisible world is also not separate from us but lies within. Various forms of contemplative practice involve awakening the connection to the invisible world. As Dante and others emphasize, contemplation requires our full attention, which we bring to our daily acts.

Some of these principles are described by Jacques Lusseryan (1987), who became blind at the age of seven and was involved in the French Resistance during the Second World War. This activity led to his internment in a German concentration camp. He survived the concentration camp and wrote the book, *And There Was Light*:

Being blind I thought I should have to go out to meet things, but I found that they came to meet me instead. I have never had to go more than halfway, and the universe became the accomplice of all my wishes ...

Touching the tomatoes in the garden, and really touching them, touching the walls of the house, the materials of the curtains or a clod of earth is surely seeing them as fully as eyes can see. But it is more than seeing them, it is tuning in on them and allowing the current they hold to connect with one's own, like electricity. To put it differently, this means an end of living in front of things and beginning of living with them. Never mind if the word sounds shocking, for this is love. (28)

Lusseryan describes so simply and vividly how to come in contact with the invisible world. Like Indigenous peoples, he sees everything as alive and having energy, and through this experience, we experience love at the most fundamental level.

By awakening to the invisible world, the healing process for the earth and ourselves can be facilitated. This healing process was described in the first chapter. Probably the greatest insight of the twelve-step program is that to heal ourselves we need to acknowledge a power greater than ourselves. Unfortunately, much of organized religion has fragmented this power and made it external to ourselves. Ultimately, we must contact this power within our own hearts. Through this act, we make the invisible world visible in our daily acts. By connecting the invisible with the visible, we start to realize a basic wholeness with ourselves and with the earth.

Chapter Six

The Mindfulness Movement

When I was writing the first edition of this book, in 1993, mindfulness as a term and practice were just beginning to be recognized. Now, mindfulness has clearly entered the mainstream. Probably the best evidence of this is Tim Ryan (2012), a United States Congressman who has written a book entitled *A Mindful Nation* (2012), which describes how mindfulness is being applied to health care, education, and even the military. When a politician embraces mindfulness and meditative practice, you realize how far the mindfulness movement has come in twenty years.

Mindfulness as a practice dates back to the Buddha (see chapter 4) and even before. It was part of the eightfold path that the Buddha introduced as a way to relieve suffering. Mindfulness has also been practised in other spiritual traditions. Consider also the words of the Monks of New Skete (1999), who are Christian:

> By training ourselves to listen attentively to what life says to us (and this means not only during meditation), we have an unparalleled opportunity to transcend self-deception, to break through our own facades, to become more deeply rooted in reality. (132)

Surely one of the goals of mindfulness practice is to "become more deeply rooted in reality."

This is the way to sanity.

In 1975, Thich Nhat Hanh, the Vietnamese monk, published *The Miracle of Mindfulness!* – one of the most important books in raising awareness about mindfulness. The book is a basic guide to mindfulness practice: "Each act must be carried out in mindfulness. Each act is a rite, a ceremony. Raising your cup of tea to your mouth is a rite" (24). In the late 1970s, the Insight Meditation Society (IMS), a meditation centre, was established in Barre, Massachusetts. Joseph Goldstein, Jack Kornfield, Sharon Salzberg, and others began offering retreats in *vipassana*, or insight meditation, that focused on developing mindful awareness. Even before the IMS was established, in 1974 Jon Kabat-Zinn went to a meditation retreat given by Joseph Goldstein and Jack Kornfield. Trained as a molecular biologist and working at the University of Massachusetts Medical Center in Worcester, he saw the potential of mindfulness practice for patients at the Center. Jon Kabat-Zinn developed the Mindfulness-Based Stress Reduction (MBSR) program for patients, which he ran in the basement of the Center. The program consisted of one day-long session and two hour-long sessions conducted over eight weeks. In 1990, Kabat-Zinn's book, *Full Catastrophe Living: Using the Wisdom of Your Body and Mind to Face Stress, Pain, and Illness*, was published that reported on his program and some of the early research showing the its positive impact. Three years later, Bill Moyers on his PBS program, *Healing the Mind*, interviewed Kabat-Zinn and that was when his work became widely recognized. Barry Boyce (2011) observes that "this was the beginning of what we now can call the "mindfulness revolution" (xiii).

MBSR is based on the assumption that people can do a lot to aid in their own healing. Kabat-Zinn in interview with me asserts, "Although we can influence healing in many ways, the ultimate capacity for healing lies within the person" (Miller 1988, 38). People referred to the program come with a variety of illnesses including cancer, heart disease, and lung disease or with lesser problems such as headaches, high blood pressure, and irritable bowel syndrome. The program takes people with whom the doctor cannot find anything wrong but who, nevertheless, are experiencing discomfort and usually a lot of anxiety. Being together in the group for eight weeks is helpful as people see they are not alone in dealing with pain. Kabat-Zinn talked to me about how mindfulness meditation is healing:

> One of the consequences of mindfulness meditation is a profound sense of relaxation. Another consequence is the falling away of personalized clinging and attachment. People see into the deeper aspects of their being and, of course, this can be very liberating. Even if people have the smallest taste of this experience it usually motivates them to go much deeper into the practice ... they usually gain something important: self-understanding and acceptance, which are fundamental to healing. (40)

Kabat-Zinn has detached MBSR from its Buddhist roots so that the language is accessible to everyone. He said to me, "Instead of talking about wisdom, generosity, attachment and non-attachment, we talk about self-confidence, self-esteem and understanding one's relationship to thought, reactivity to stressful situations, how reactivity and unmindful thought can make us anxious" (41).

People who work in his program need to be deeply involved in their own practice. Kabat-Zinn told me that he believes that the "program comes from our own guts and practice ... if the program does not come from your own work on yourself, then you will not be able to respond to other people and the variety of questions that arise" (42). It is also important in the program that the leaders avoid language or behaviour that can lead to a sense of us and them. Kabat-Zinn says, "We try to view the participant simply as people like ourselves" (44); thus, medical terms such as "liver patient" or "low back patient" are avoided.

There have been studies conducted on the impact of MBSR. Daniel Siegel (2011) summarizes some of this research. First, MBSR training enhances left frontal activity in the brain, which apparently aids people in "moving towards, rather than away from a challenging external situation." It supports what is called an "approach state" that can be seen "as the neural basis of resilience" (138). Second, this change in the brain is also associated with an improvement in the immune system and the ability to fight infection. Third, the research on MBSR shows that "patients feel an internal sense of stability and clarity" (138–9). This helps adults and adolescents with attention difficulties to improve their ability to sustain concentration. In this regard, MBSR was found to be even more effective than medications. Fourth, MBSR has helped in dealing with a number of mental health difficulties including "obsessive-compulsive disorder, borderline personality disorder, drug addiction and in the prevention of chronically relapsing depression" (139). Mindfulness meditation helps the person discern different thoughts, and this is a crucial step in "disentangling the mind from ruminative thoughts, repetitive emotions, and impulsive and addictive behaviors" (139). Kabat-Zinn (Miller 1988) elaborates on this:

> When we get angry or fearful about a situation, it can make things even worse. However, through meditation you can systematically see the thoughts and the emotional reactions and you can begin to uncouple the thoughts from the pain. If you can uncouple the thoughts from the pain, you can reduce symptoms associated with pain 15 to 40 percent. Relaxation can bring about another 15 to 40 percent. We are working to just allow the pain to be as it is unaccompanied by cognitive and emotional baggage. At this point we

have had numerous people experience the whole thing just falling away. Either the pain disappears or if it is still there, it doesn't feel like pain anymore because all the labels associated with it are gone. To be free of pain for only a short time can be very liberating and encourages the person to go deeper into practice. (47).

I asked Jon Kabat-Zinn what he had learned from his patients:

I have learned how powerful people are when they are given permission to experiment and ask questions about who they really are. I am very moved when I hear from people how simply paying attention can be so healing.

I have learned from them what is possible for a human being to do. The story is always the same; we start with a group that really doesn't know why they are there and over the eight weeks it is miraculous to watch what happens. There are miracles of growth, understanding, letting go of one's defenses, becoming more honest and caring for oneself. The last miracle is especially important because these people are often very hard on themselves. (47)

The MBSR program has now spread around the world and is given a variety of settings. Boyce (2011) writes that these variations include "Mindfulness-Based Childbirth and Parenting, Mindfulness-Based Cognitive Therapy, Mindfulness-Based Eating Awareness Training, and Mindfulness-Based Art Training for Cancer Patients" (xiii). Other mindfulness-based programs include the Mindfulness Awareness Research Center (MARC) at the University of California–Los Angeles (UCLA). Susan Smalley and Diana Winston (2010), who work there, have written what in my view is one of the best books on mindfulness, *Fully Present: The Science, Art and Practice of Mindfulness*. Smalley is a researcher in the area of mindfulness while Winston is a mindfulness teacher. Together they present both the research on mindfulness as well as a variety of mindfulness exercises that the reader can practise.

Business

Mindfulness practices have found their way into a variety of areas including business, health care, law, and education. One of the most interesting examples from the business world is at Google, where Chade-meng Tan (2012) has developed a mindfulness program for employees. He describes this program in his book, *Search Inside Yourself: Google's Guide to Enhancing Productivity, Creativity and Happiness*. The program was developed in collaboration with Daniel Goleman so that Goleman's work in emotional intelligence could be integrated into the program. One suggestion that Norman Fischer (2011) makes, who also works at Google, is to be mindful when sending an e-mail. He writes, "Instead of shooting off a hurried e-mail and dealing with the consequences later, take an extra moment. Write the e-mail, then close your eyes and visualize the person who is going to receive it. Remember that he or she is alive, a feeling human being. Now go back and re-read the e-mail, changing anything you now feel you want to change before sending it" (54).

Lewis Richmond is an ordained disciple of Shunryu Suzuki Roshi, who spent the first fifteen years of his adult life as a Buddhist priest and meditation teacher and the second fifteen years as a business executive and entrepreneur. In 1999, his book, *Work as Spiritual Practice: A Practical Buddhist Approach to Inner Growth and Satisfaction on the Job*, was published. It is one of the best books on how one can bring a contemplative perspective into the workplace. Richmond says "spiritual practice is a way to transform the mundane into the sacred, the ordinary into the profound" (11). He goes on to describe the nature of spiritual practice as "something we DO (as opposed to something we believe) that helps us" confront such basic questions as, What is my purpose? Spiritual practice "is an activity that changes us inside, that reverberates in the soul" (14).

Richmond gives many examples of spiritual practice. One is a story about Harry Roberts, who was part Irish and part Native American. As a small boy, Harry watched his uncle sewing feathers into a headdress. At one point, he took a whole section out and sewed it again. Harry asked his uncle why he did this because no one would see as it was going to be used at night. Harry asked, "Who will know?" His uncle replied, "I will know." Richmond concludes, "Sewing the headdress was not about stitches or embroidery. It was about spirit, about responsibility, and about character. It was spiritual practice" (15).

Richmond acknowledges the challenges of applying spiritual practice to the workplace but writes, "No matter how insecure our tenure at work, no one can hand a pink slip to our soul. No one can say to our inner life, 'You're fired!' I will say it again: You are the boss of your inner life" (20). Richmond includes chapters on conflict, worry, anger, boredom, failure, discouragement, ambition, money, forgiveness, quitting, generosity, and gratitude. There is also a chapter on meditation, which has some of the meditations described in chapter 3 of this book. He has one entitled "Sitting Meditation at Work." In this meditation, start by putting both feet flat on the floor and letting your hands rest on your lap or armrests. Then take ten deep breaths. Richmond recommends doing this once every hour, or eight times a day. If you are sitting in front of the computer, he suggests looking about an inch below the screen. You can also put the computer on sleep and contemplate the blank screen for a minute or so. At the end of each chapter, Richmond gives a few specific suggestions. For example, in the chapter on generosity, there are these practices:

- When you are listening to someone, see if you can notice the shift between hearing with the ear and Hearing with the Heart. What is the difference?
- Remember the gift of Presence. Just to be there is the most fundamental generosity of all.
- Practice kindness, particularly when you feel irritated or things are not going well. Kindness hardly every goes wrong.
- Pay attention to what you say and how you say it. Can you practice Right Speech as conscious speech? Even a critical comment can contain some element of generosity. (214)

My wife is Japanese and my connection with her culture has led me to appreciate the importance of saying "*arigato*" or "thank you." Richmond writes that there is a movement whose main spiritual practice is to say "Thank you!" with as much sincerity as possible. In this movement, the two words are seen as a universal prayer.

Law

Law is another profession that has begun using mindfulness. Charles Halpern, who has been practising meditation since the early 1980s when he was the dean of City University of New York's law school, has been leading a weekly meditation group at the law school at the University of California–Berkeley with the director of the law program there (Boyce 2011, 260).

Jon Kabat-Zinn gave a course to judges in Massachusetts. He told me, "They have to sit all day, but have they ever had any training in sitting: Of course not. As judges they are supposed to demonstrate equanimity, compassion and discriminating wisdom and again they never have had any systematic training in any of these areas" (Miller 1988, 45). Later, he heard that one of the judges in his program had introduced mindfulness awareness to the jury in his instructions. The judge had said to the jury, "I want you to pay attention from moment to moment to moment. It is important" (Kabat-Zinn 2005, 455).

Sports

Mindfulness has become part of the sports world, particularly through the work of Phil Jackson, who has coached the Chicago Bulls and the Los Angeles Lakers in the National Basketball Association. His book, *Sacred Hoops: Spiritual Lessons of a Hardwood Warrior* (1995), describes how he introduced mindfulness to his players so that they could go beyond ego and become a real team. In the first few pages of the book, he writes:

> When players practice what is known as mindfulness – simply paying atten-
> tion to what's actually happening – not only do they play better and win
> more, they also become more attuned with each other. And the joy they ex-
> perience working in harmony is a powerful motivating force that comes
> from deep within, not from some frenzied coach pacing along the sidelines,
> shouting obscenities into the air. (6)

Jackson has done Zen meditation, which provided the foundation of bringing mindfulness into his coaching. He was also influenced by Shunryu Suzuki Roshi as he used his book, *Zen Mind, Beginner's Mind*, as his guide to practice. Jackson (1995) found the following results of introducing meditation to his players: "The experience of sitting silently together in a group tends to bring about a subtle shift in consciousness that strengthens the team bond. Sometimes we extend mindfulness to the courts and conduct whole practices in silence" (119). Some of his players talked about the importance of *not thinking, just doing* when they are on the court: "The game happens so fast, the less I can think and the more I can just react to what's going on, the better it will be for me and, ulti-mately, the team" (120).

Another professional athlete who has written about mindfulness in sports is the baseball player Shawn Green (2011). Unlike Jackson, Green did not have formal training in meditation. Instead, when he was struggling with his hitting, he started to practice swinging his bat at a batting tee:

> My mantra was the ball motionless; the only movement I focused on was the
> movement of my breath. The swing occurred on it own. Absorbed in the
> action of hitting, I felt my body moving, I saw only the ball, and I heard the

contact of the wood on the ball followed by the swishing sound of the ball hitting the back of the cage – a beautiful practice.

I had reduced hitting, an extremely difficult activity, to its most basic form. As a result, I took each swing with full attention. (20)

Green also developed a technique to bring him out of his head and into his body. He would tap the bat on the cleats of his shoes in order "to move awareness into my feet, and out of my *mind*" (62, original emphasis). For Green, when awareness is "placed in the body, *presence* emerges" (121, emphasis added). Green also writes about how his awareness went beyond baseball into his whole life. The last chapter in his book is entitled "Gratitude," where he writes about the importance of being with his young family after retiring from playing. He looked forward to embracing a "heightened state of awareness in his new life" (220–1). For Green, "life is really just one beautiful moment constantly changing shape" (200).

David Forbes (2004) has worked with high school football players, and he introduced them to mindfulness meditation. He also conducted research on this work. He describes his overall approach at the beginning of his book, *Boyz 2 Buddhas: Counseling Urban High School Male Athletes in the Zone.* He writes, "An important theme of the book is that meditation promotes spiritual well-being, which is associated with less rigid adherence to stereotypical masculinity, which is stressful" (5). Forbes was not just interested in the boys becoming better football players but in their overall development. Forbes did research on this project and found some positive results. For example, he found that the boys became more mindful of "feelings like hurt and anger, of hurtful behaviors, and of the need to take responsibility for one's feelings" (164).

Education

Mindfulness has been adopted in a variety of educational settings. I met Linda Lantieri at Findhorn in 2000 at a conference on Education and the Soul. She had been working in New York City schools for several years around conflict resolution and peace education. The next year was 9/11, which happened near her office in New York City. Since then she has developed the Inner Resilience Program. This program combines mindfulness meditation with social emotional learning (SEL) to help children and adolescents cope with stresses in their lives as well to enhance their ability to focus and learn in school. At the invitation of Congressman Tim Ryan, she brought the program to Youngstown and Warren school districts in Ohio. The website for the program states, "Since we began this work in 2002, we have served over 5,000 school staff, 2,000 parents and over 10,000 students, who have helped to reclaim their schools as caring communities of learning" (http://www.innerresilience-tidescenter.org/).

Several studies have been conducted on the program indicating its positive impact. One included 57 teachers and 855 students in New York City classrooms (Grades 3–5). Linda Lantieri reports:

> Between-group analyses indicated several interesting and notable results with regard to teacher wellness, including reduced stress levels (as measured by one scale), increased levels of attention and mindfulness, and greater perceived relational trust among treatment teachers. Additionally, 3rd-grade students of treatment teachers perceived that they had significantly more autonomy and influence in their classes at the end of the school year than at the beginning, and analyses of student wellness indicated that the program had a significant, positive impact on reducing 3rd- and 4th-grade students' frustration levels. (http://www.lindalantieri.org/links_irp.htm)

The Mind-Body Awareness (MBA) program in Oakland California developed by Noah Levine works with inner city youth, often gang members. Director of the MBA Chris McKenna introduces mindfulness activities through martial arts movies and songs to engage the young people. McKenna says, "I've experienced many different approaches to working with people in these kinds of extreme circumstances and mindfulness is by far the most powerful intervention I've ever worked with" (cited in Boyce 2011, 257).

Another program that is being used in North America is the MindUP program developed by the Goldie Hawn Foundation. The website describes the program: "MindUP™ is a family of social, emotional, and attentional self-regulatory strategies and skills developed for cultivating well-being and emotional balance. Among the various MindUP™ skills taught to students, focused attention and nonreactive monitoring of experience from moment to moment display the potential to have a long-term impact on brain function and social and emotional behavior" (www.thehawnfoundation.org/mindup).

The following are some of the self-reported changes from students in the MindUP™ program:

• Increased empathy
• Significant rise in optimism
• Increased emotional control

- Improved focused attention
- Working more collaboratively with classmates. (thehawnfoundation.org/mindup/)

Geoffrey Soloway, one of my former doctoral students, conducted his doctoral research on mindfulness in teacher education. Along with others, he developed a course for teachers in the Initial Teacher Education Program at the Ontario Institute for Studies in Education at the University of Toronto. This course uses MBSR, supplemented with a wellness component enhancing the well-being of the student teachers. It also focuses on how mindfulness strategies could be introduced in the classroom, so it has a pedagogical focus as well. The course is called Mindfulness-Based Wellness Education (MBWE), and its primary objectives are to help teacher candidates do the following:

1 Enhance their ability to respond (versus react) to stressful situations both within and outside of the classroom in order to reduce their levels of stress and improve their health
2 Explore their understanding and experience of various aspects of wellness
3 Learn teaching strategies for bringing mindfulness and wellness into their classrooms. (Soloway, Poulin, and Mackenzie 2010, 221)

The first objective is met through various strategies used in the MBSR program including mindful sitting and the body scan. Mindful yoga is also used. Students are encouraged to be mindful in their daily activities and to be aware of their thoughts and emotions. The wellness component is developed through a wellness wheel that has seven dimensions of wellness including the physical, emotional, social, mental, ecological, vocational, and spiritual. The students work through these dimensions throughout the course focusing on a different dimension each week. The third objective is met by discussing mindful teaching strategies that could be used in the classroom.

In the study, the student teachers were interviewed to assess the effects of the practice. It was found that it helped them in their teaching practicum in the schools to be more relaxed. One person said:

My attitude and mind-set can be picked up by the students and when I present myself as a balanced and mindful teacher, the students will respond in a calmer manner. The basics of this course can be used to approach classroom management from an entirely different perspective. (Soloway, Poulin, and Mackenzie 2010, 224)

In some cases, it led to deeper reflection and transformation:

> Often people say, "practice makes perfect." In this course we have learned that "practice allows us not to be perfect." From this course and its practices and concepts I have been able to understand that [by] being mindful throughout my life, I can embrace both the positive and negative events that happen. This allows me to continually learn, a concept that summarizes education in its simplest form. (Ibid.)

Overall, it was found that those enrolled in the course exhibited significantly greater increases in mindfulness, life satisfaction, and teaching self-efficacy. A complete report on the quantitative and qualitative evaluation of MBWE can be found in a study by Poulin, Mackenzie, Soloway, and Karaoylas (2008).

THE GARRISON INSTITUTE

The Garrison Institute was founded in 2003 and has provided leadership in contemplative education and mindfulness training. It sees its role in nurturing contemplative education through "supporting the leaders, providing a network and a collaborative hub for those pursuing high quality, evidence-based work in the field" (Jennings and Rome 2011, 251). One of the priorities is the Initiative on Contemplation and Education (ICE), which has sponsored a number of forums and conferences on Contemplative Education. I attended one in January 2012 that focused on teacher education and included twenty teacher educators from North America. The long-term goals of ICE include:

1 Building the knowledge base
2 Developing infrastructure for collaboration and information exchange
3 Codifying standards of practice
4 Generating resources (funding, etc.)
5 Strengthening the workforce and leadership
6 Cultivating the grassroots and policy climate. (Jennings and Rome 2011, 252)

In 2005, the Garrison Institute published the first mapping survey of the field that identified emerging practices and a preliminary theoretical framework. Their CARE (Cultivating Awareness and Resilience in Education) program is a teacher-training curriculum, to which mindfulness activities are central:

Based upon current research on the neuroscience of emotion, CARE intro-duces emotion skills instruction to promote understanding, recognition and regulation of emotion. To reduce stress, and to promote awareness and pres-ence applied to teaching, CARE introduces basic mindfulness activities such as short periods of silent reflection, and progresses to activities that demon-strate how to bring mindfulness to challenging situations teachers often en-counter. Through these activities, teachers learn to bring greater calm, mind-fulness and awareness into the classroom to enhance their relationships with their students, their classroom management, and curricular implementation. The CARE program also promotes empathy and compassion through caring practice and mindful listening activities. (http://www.garrisoninstitute.org/contemplation-and-education/care-for-teachers)

This program helps teachers to be aware of their reactions and to see students in a more compassionate way. Tish Jennings, the director of CARE says, "If teachers can notice the emotion within their body, they can stop and make choices. Instead of seeing children with challenging behavior as problems, they can experience them as suffering human beings who need compassion. Over time, that will change how they lead their classrooms" (cited in Ryan 2012, 82). Research has been conducted on CARE and the following results have been reported: There were significant improvements in well-being, efficacy, and mindfulness among teachers who participated in CARE compared with the control group. These results are reported in a paper presented at the 2012 annual meeting of the American Education Research Association (Jennings, Snowberg, Coccia and Greenberg 2012).

Two books worth noting for teachers are *Mindful Teaching and Teach-ing Mindfulness: A Guide for Anyone who Teaches Anything* (2009), by Deborah Shoeberlein, and *Child's Mind: Mindfulness Practices to Help Our Children Be More Focused, Calm, and Relaxed* (2010), by Christo-pher Willard. Both books are clearly written and include a variety of exer-cises that teachers can use with students and to be more present in the classroom.

THE CENTER FOR CONTEMPLATIVE MIND IN SOCIETY

While the Garrison Institute focuses primarily on elementary and second-ary school education, the Center for Contemplative Mind in Society has a program in higher education – the Association for Contemplative Mind in Higher Education (ACMHE):

The mission of the ACMHE is to advocate for contemplative practice in higher education; to encourage new forms of inquiry and imaginative thinking; and to educate active citizens who will support a more just and compassionate direction for society. The ACMHE supports members in the development of contemplative pedagogy, research methodology, epistemology and organizational designs by creating forums for the exchange of diverse perspectives on contemplative practice in higher education. It supports the creation of a community of contemplative educators, scholars, administrators and students to develop a broad culture of contemplation in the academy. (http://www.contemplativemind.org/programs/acmhe)

Mirabai Bush (2011), the founding director of the Center, has written about some of its activities. In 1997, the Center, in partnership with the American Council of Learned Societies, began to offer fellowships to professors who were interested in including contemplation in their courses. The first year, they received 136 applications and sixteen fellowships were awarded to help "create curriculum in diverse disciplines that encompass and encourage the study of contemplation" (229). By 2010, there were 158 fellows in more than a hundred colleges and universities. Professional schools that have developed contemplative programs include Brown Medical School, University of Massachusetts Medical School, Harvard Law School, and the University of California–Berkeley Boalt Hall School of Law. Mindfulness is also taught at the Peter Drucker Graduate School of Management at Claremont. Smith College of Social Work has begun a "paradigm-shifting initiative in American social work education, the program considers the clinical relationship as a potential locus of the sacred" (252).

MY OWN WORK WITH MINDFULNESS

Since 1988 I have introduced meditation and mindfulness practices to students in my graduate courses and Initial Teacher Education courses. Most of these students are experienced teachers or teachers in training. I review some of this work in the last chapter but I can only agree with Jon Kabat-Zinn that after being together for twelve weeks little miracles occur. I would like to cite the example of two students who integrated mindfulness into their lives.

Mona. Mona comes from a Muslim country, Kuwait. When she was living in England during the Gulf War in 1991 she volunteered to teach people in her own Kuwaiti community. She also taught family and friends when they needed help. Since she came to Canada, she has taught ESL for people in her community. Now, she is focusing on learning to play piano and music theory.

She uses walking meditation and breathing meditation, repeats mantras, and tries to bring mindfulness into her daily life. Much of her practice focuses on mindfulness, which she has found very helpful in practising the piano. Mona comments:

> The mindfulness really helps, because it is simple and can be an integral part of whatever I'm doing, for instance, in my piano practice. When I am present with the notes I play, I can hear them better, which brings me deep joy and helps me in knowing what needs to be improved. I drift off, of course, but then I bring myself back.

In her personal life, Mona points out that her family was influenced by her meditation practices as she and her husband have learned mindfulness together:

> My husband was enlightened by many of the things I learned and I passed on to him. He helps me a lot in his own way ... we learned the mindfulness together. He easily incorporates it in his daily activity.

Her husband said that she is changing a lot from what she used to be as he has been observing the changes through time. She used to worry a lot, and now she is trying to focus on the moment rather than being absent-minded and anxious. When she went back to Kuwait, a few of her family members noted that she seemed more relaxed and happier. She was amused that the changes in her personality were noticed:

> It changed my life a lot in many ways from the inside. I know I'm less anxious and worried, and whenever I let my mind dwell on the future or the past, I get upset again, and then I have to bring myself back. When I'm thinking of the past or the future, and they are equally painful ... I can simply bring myself to the present with a few breaths, breathing deeply, and then focusing on the moment and just doing it without letting thought distract me; that's very helpful for me.

Mona is more mindful now, and she finds it easier to be present. She reminds herself whenever her mind drifts off to come back to the present. The more she becomes mindful, the easier it gets to include mindfulness in her daily activities. She thinks that it is our nature to be in the moment as young children are naturally mindful. As people get older, there is tendency to seek approval that can make us anxious, unsettled, and not present. Mona believes that mindfulness helps us to let go of the need to meet other people's expectations. She explains that the element of the practice is simplicity, which we cannot complicate by using a lot of words. Mona's next comment describes that the important lesson is in the experience itself:

> I don't need to even describe it, that's the good part. We understand it and we do it. Quieting the mind, actually, is very important. I don't think we have to, though. It's not, 'have to.' Because that's what brought me to trouble in the first place. The 'Have to,' or 'I should do this or that'... If any thought comes in, you don't force it out, you let it smoothly go out. It's not having to or forcing something.

What Mona says relates to accepting what seem to be obstacles. She talks about accepting herself:

> It's OK ... that's one of the things I'm beginning to tell myself. It's very powerful thing for me. When I make a mistake, I am very critical about myself, and this is what I'm changing, and I know it's in the process. I'm telling myself it is OK when I make mistakes.

She adds that allowing ourselves to be who we are can be difficult:

> Sometimes we need permission from others to allow ourselves to rest and be who we are. This is very difficult ... I don't allow myself, and I know many don't also. It's very hard.

Meditation seems to help in the process of accepting ourselves. Finally, Mona comments on the relation between her faith and the mindfulness practice:

> In Islam, there are many instructions that Muslims are encouraged to do. For example, when we want to enter the bathroom, it's encouraged to enter with the right foot first, and say a kind of short prayer ... I believe that these little prayers and acts are a way to stay present, to be mindful of what we're doing. So, I think that mindfulness is an integral part of any religion.

Mona has found that mindfulness supports her religious practice.

Astrid. While Mona focused on how mindfulness has affected her personal life, Astrid wrote about how she brought mindfulness into her teaching day. I have cited this in some of my other works (Miller 2006, 2007) and again here because it is such beautiful example of how mindfulness can be part of a teacher's day:

I began each day marveling at the miracle of life, of falling asleep and awakening to a wondrous world. With this thought, I began my morning rituals. Thinking of my daily routines as rituals actually helped me in attaining a more aware state as I washed my face, took my shower, ate my breakfast and walked (or drove) to work. Upon entering the school, I decided to go to my classroom first. I had previously been going into the office to sign in and say good morning, etc. but this took away form the oneness that I needed in my "mindfulness" training. I ritualized all my tasks – walking up the stairs, putting the key into the classroom door, hanging up my coat, etc. It was actually amazing how being mindful of these simple tasks allowed me to begin my day in a calm clear and less cluttered way. How many times had I come into this room, dumped my coat, hat and mitts on my chair, ran to the photocopy room and back, spent another half-hour looking for the photocopying I had laid down somewhere, not to mention the frantic search for mitts when it was time to go out on duty? Instead, I began to become aware of my mornings in the classroom and in turn they became calm and focused.

My most favorite part of this pre-school ritual is writing the schedule on the board. My team teacher had tried to talk me out of this last June (she writes the daily schedule for each day on the sheets of chart paper and laminates them). At the time, I explained to her that writing the schedule on the board had many different purposes for me. The most important one was that it allowed me to center myself in the classroom. I look back now on how intuitive I had been and I am amazed. Being mindful of this particular ritual has made me fully aware of the "here" during the hectic day. I stand at the front of the room and feel the smooth texture of the chalk in my hands. I think about where I am and I observe my surroundings – the plants, the books, the desks, the children's slippers – I am, for the second time that day, amazed at the miracle of life.

The days begins, I stand outside the classroom fully aware of each individual as they enter the room. I interact with them, I say hello, it feels good. This is new, until now, I had never made it to the door when the children entered – I was always too busy! I try to maintain this sense of awareness – aware of my feelings (physical and emotional) and my reactions to the things that are happening "now." Of course, the craziness of the classroom day begins and it becomes more and more difficult to maintain this awareness as the day wears on. However, now instead of working through recess,

I take the time to visit with colleagues in the staff room. When I can, I take a walk down to the beach at lunch and look out across the lake, mindful of the beauty of the world around me. When the day ends, I recapture this mindful state and fully participate in the end-of-day ritual with my students. After the children have left, I sweep the floor, being mindful of my movements and the sound of the broom. I often begin by thinking that I am sweeping the day's events away and that I am focusing on the "now" – the actual act of sweeping. The pleasure of being here, and being able to fully participate reminds me again of the miracle of life.

Each of my students has worked with mindfulness in her or his own way. One of the beauties of the practice is that it is *organic*. So much of education has tended towards strategies that are formulistic and mechanical, but this practice can be life giving. My favourite definition of mindfulness comes from Susan Murphy (2006), a Zen teacher in Australia, who has put it like this: "A most simple definition of mindful behavior is paying attention. This gives beauty to all things; they feel attended to" (19). One can feel the beauty in Mona's and Astrid's approach to mindfulness.

Chapter Seven

What I Have Learned/Jack's Journey

What I Have Learned

In 1988, I started including a meditation component in my graduate classes in education. I teach courses in Holistic Education and Spirituality in Education at the Ontario Institute for Studies in Education at the University of Toronto. In this chapter, I reflect on what I have learned from working with contemplative practices for over twenty years.

Rationale

I believe it is important for the reader to know a little about my own practice, and more importantly, my rationale for including contemplative practices in my classes. My own practice is *vipassana*, or insight meditation, which is described in chapter 3. Vipassana focuses on developing awareness and being present in the moment. I started this as daily practice in 1974, and my first teacher – through taped instructions – was Joseph Goldstein (1976). Today, my teachers are Norman Feldman and Molly Swan, who teach for True North Insight, and I try to attend one of their seven-day retreats every year. Although vipassana is my core practice, I have also done mantra and occasionally do image work.

My rationale for including meditation in my classes includes several points. Most of my students are teachers who are taking graduate courses in education, so my rationale focuses on teacher development. Perhaps most important is the concept of teacher presence, which I also discussed in chapter 1. Teaching, in my view, involves three basic factors. First is the theory or assumptions underlying our approach to teaching; the underlying assumptions and theories have been referred to as "orientations" (Eisner and Vallance 1974; Miller 1983). Second are the teaching strategies and practices that we employ in the classroom. Also included here are the evaluation methods used to assess student development. The final factor is the presence of the teacher. This last factor is so critical. If we recall the teachers that have had an impact on us, usually it is not the material that they taught that we remember but that elusive quality of presence that somehow touched us.

The Zen Roshi, Shunryu Suzuki, tells a wonderful story about the presence of a teacher (Chadwick 1999). He was head of a temple in Japan and was looking for a kindergarten teacher for the temple school. He repeatedly tried to convince a woman to take the job but she refused. Finally, he said to her, "You don't have to do anything, just stand there." When he said that, she accepted the position. He was convinced that her presence alone would make a difference in the lives of the children. Of course, she did not just stand in the classroom but Shunryu Suzuki Roshi identified this important element in teaching.

Teacher presence is often ignored in teacher education as the focus tends to be on theory and teaching strategies; yet, teacher presence is critically important, particularly in holistic education.

Presence and being in the moment mean that there is less chance that we will be teaching from our egos. If teaching is ego-based, it can become a frustrating series of mini-battles with students. The classroom becomes focused around the issue of control. If we teach from that place where we are present and attentive, teaching can become a more fulfilling and enriching experience. Robert Griffin (1977) summarizes this very well:

> You do not feel set off against them [the students] or competitive with them. You see yourself in students and them in you. You move easily, are more relaxed, and seem less threatening to students. You are less compulsive, less rigid in your thoughts and actions. You are not so tense. You do not seem to be in a grim win-or-lose contest when teaching. (79)

Another important reason is that contemplation is basically a form of self-learning. Through the process of contemplation, one learns to trust one's own deeper intuitive responses. For example, insight meditation is based on the notion that we can learn and grow by simply mindfully watching our own experience. As we notice our own thoughts and agendas, we can gain deeper insight into ourselves and the nature of the mind-body experience. In contrast, the model for most learning at the university level is that the professor and the text are the sources of learning and the student must learn from these external authorities. Contemplation provides one alternative to this model and, instead, recognizes that we can learn from our own direct experience.

A final reason for engaging in contemplation is that it allows teachers to deal with the stresses in their lives. Teaching can be a very stressful profession. Research indicates that meditation is an effective tool in the relaxation process (Smalley and Winston 2010), and given the pressures that teachers face today, this aspect of contemplation should not be overlooked. The vast majority of students in my classes have seen the positive effects of contemplative practice in having fewer headaches and simply being able to address stressful events that come up in their lives and in the classroom. One of my students was a secondary school vice-principal who faced many stressful events during the day. He wrote in his journal that as the pressures of his job increased he found that he needed to engage in meditation more frequently. Teachers also found that they were less reactive in the classroom.

The Process

In two of my graduate courses, and in one Initial Teacher Education course, I require students to meditate daily for six weeks; in another course, it is an option. In the graduate courses, where it is required, I introduce the practice in the third week of classes. I first offer a definition of meditation, which is the development of compassionate attention, and then I present the rationale for doing meditation, which was described above. I then introduce them to eight different types of meditation. We spend approximately two minutes doing each one. I suggest that they choose one to work with for the six weeks. These methods were described in the chapter 3 and include:

- *Observing the breath*. The student observes the breath, focusing on either the nostrils or the rising and falling of the belly.
- *Counting the breath*. The student counts each exhalation, starting with the first and finishing with the fourth exhalation. In both these breath exercises, I note that the student should not try to control the process but breathe naturally.
- *Body scan*. The student mindfully scans the body from head to foot and then foot to head.
- *Mantra*. A sound or phrase is repeated silently.

- *Visualization*. The student visualizes a series of images, usually from an experience in nature.
- *Walking*. This practice focuses the awareness on the foot leaving and touching the ground.
- *Contemplation*. The student selects a short passage of poetry or inspirational text and repeats it silently.
- *Loving-kindness*. Thoughts of well-being are sent first to ourselves and then to others.

If any students already have a practice, I do not ask them to change what they are doing. Students are asked to start meditating five to ten minutes a day and over the course of the six weeks gradually work up to twenty or thirty minutes. Some students are able to begin with twenty minutes a day. They keep a daily journal describing how the process is going, and they are asked to report on what the body is experiencing during the meditation and what was prominent during the practice (e.g., thoughts, sounds, etc.). Below is one example of a daily entry:

Aug 2nd Observing the Breath

Profoundly noticeable a number of times during this session was the wave of relaxation moving thought my legs from top to bottom. I could feel the tension leaving the body, flowing out through the tips of my toes. Other thoughts came and went as I attempted to return to the breathing and the awareness of my chest moving up and down. My hands melted into my knees. I felt rejuvenated and ready for the rest of the evening.

I encourage students also to submit questions to me in their journals if any issues arise during their practice. At the end of the six weeks, they write a one- or two-page summary reflection on their practice. Here are the reflections of one woman that also include how she brought her practice into her teaching:

Through daily meditation, I have been able to take some time for myself in order to relax, regain a sense of who I am and my physical needs. I have taken the opportunity to meditate daily for the past six weeks (and counting) in order to take into consideration the simple things that I can do for myself to help myself feel better, such as breathing properly and taking time to really enjoy little things that I experience, as opposed to moving on to the next thing without appreciating what I've just seen or felt.

I found that the energy that was generated from my meditative experience stayed with me for much of the day. I have felt great over these past couple of months and have attributed much of that to the feeling of comfort with myself and a positive outlook on things. I really have felt that meditation has had an impact on my relationships with others. My attention seemed more focused at work and in my personal life following meditation.

The relationship that I have had with my class has been a close one, yet I feel that our class meditations have brought many of us much closer. My students write journal entries about finding their "star" and going to their "garden" as they meditate on their own at home (often at bedtime as they begin their dreams!). One seven-year-old student's reflection that really stands out to me is that "meditation makes me feel kind of in between" not happy or sad, "just calm." This, with the added energy and an overall sense of satisfaction with life, seemed to sum it up for me, too.

Some of themes that run through the journals include:

- Giving permission to be alone and enjoy one's own company
- Increased listening capacities
- Feeling increased energy
- Being less reactive to situations and generally experiencing greater calm and clarity.

There are two other elements that are included in my classes. I begin each class with the loving-kindness meditation that was described in chapter 3.

The third element that I include is introducing the students to mindfulness practice in daily life. This means being attentive and present to activities during the day. Students first experience the raisin exercise described in chapter 3. I then encourage them to start with one daily activity (e.g., doing the dishes, preparing a meal, brushing the teeth) and to do it without thinking about something else. Beginning with simple daily tasks can build a foundation of mindfulness that can eventually extend to the classroom so that teachers can be more present to their students. One former student describes mindfulness experiences:

I find these little moments kind of funny when they happen because all of a sudden I become very aware that I'm washing the dishes or vacuuming ... And I kind of get into the moment, and it stays with me during the day." (Female adminstrator)

The students in my graduate classes are mostly teachers working in public or Catholic schools. About 70%–80% are women, and the ages range from the mid-twenties to the fifties. Toronto has been identified as the most multicultural city in the world, and my classes reflect that diversity. Students from Brazil, China, Egypt, Indonesia, Iran, Italy, Jamaica, Japan, Kenya, Korea, Lebanon, Malta, Serbia, Tibet, Ukraine, and Vietnam have been in my classes. The average class size is around twenty-four students. To date, approximately two thousand students have been introduced to meditation practice in my courses. Only three students have asked not to do the assignment as one student had been sexually abused a year before and did not feel comfortable with the practice. The other student was a Christian fundamentalist. The third student was a woman whose husband had left her during the course. So far there has not been a student who has reported an overall negative experience with the practice during the course.

Research

A few years ago, together with my graduate assistant, I conducted a study as a follow-up of people who had done the meditation in one of the courses mentioned above and had continued with their practice (Miller and Nozawa 2002). The study focused on the following questions:

1 What is the nature of your meditation practice? (e.g., type and frequency)
2 Have you engaged in any meditation instruction since the class?
3 What have been the effects of your practice on your personal and professional life?
4 Have you experienced any difficulties or problems with the practice?

Letters were sent out to 182 former students asking if they would be interested in participating in an interview related to the questions above. Because the study involved a face-to-face interview, the study was limited to former students living in the Toronto area. From this group, forty letters were returned, because many students had moved. In the end, twenty-one former students (17 women and 4 men) agreed to participate. Of these twenty-one, eleven were teachers at the elementary or secondary level, four were teaching at the post-secondary level, four were administrators, and two were consultants.

The participants were interviewed by my graduate assistant, Ayako Nozawa. The interview lasted between thirty minutes and an hour and a half. To triangulate the data, the following material was also collected:

1 Meditation journals from the course
2 Summary reflections on the meditation submitted as part of the course
3 The interviewer's reflections on the interviews.

Effects of Meditation Practice

All the participants except one commented on the positive effects of the practice on their personal and professional lives.

PERSONAL EFFECTS

The majority of participants (13, or 62%) commented on how the meditation had helped them become calmer and more relaxed. One female nursing instructor commented:

> I'm not as agitated … or I'm not as arousable from the point of view that things don't bother me as much … I feel calmer, I feel more … this word centered keeps coming to mind.

Another main effect (noted by five participants) was that they felt the meditation softened them or made them more gentle. One woman stated:

> It made a difference in softening me in my home, in my personal life in terms of working through the process with my husband and, you know, how do you solve this?" (Female principal)

Finally, five participants felt that the meditation had helped them with personal relationships. One female administrator commented, "It affects all your relationships. They're better. They're deeper." A male consultant found that people come to him for help:

> Well a lot of my friends, they phone me for advice. I'm sort of like their counselor, because once you get into that whole realm of awareness and meditation and looking at things in perspective …

PROFESSIONAL EFFECTS

Again, more than half of the participants commented on how the meditation helped them be calmer in the workplace. One principal commented on how calmness is important to the whole process of change:

> And to get any kind of change happening in schools, it's imperative that people are calm and are in an almost meditative state in order to make those changes that are being demanded.

This principal runs meetings that don't have an agenda so that "we're just here to talk about the work that we're doing, and enjoy each other." She adds this is "not team building, it's just kind of being together, it doesn't have a name."

A related effect is that the participants commented that they are not as reactive as they step back from troublesome situations:

> You can get really frustrated with these kids because these kids get really angry and frustrated because they can't read, and your first response is to be an authoritarian, when actually they just need to be hugged and loved. So it [the meditation] really helps me to step back and look at what really is going on. (Female teacher)

Another teacher simply said, "I don't remember the last time I raised my voice." She added that one of her students said to her, "Miss, how come you're so calm all the time?"

A large amount of data supporting the effectiveness of meditation has been collected (Kabat-Zinn 2005; Smalley and Winston 2010). These benefits include physical ones such as lowering blood pressure and cholesterol levels. Mindfulness-Based Stress Reduction programs have also shown improvements in physical and mental health measures; some of this research was summarized in chapter 6. Recent research has focused on the brain, and one study shows structural changes in the brain as a result of meditation and that these changes are associated with improvements in mental health (Davidson and Begley 2012). Studies have found that meditation can increase creativity, academic achievement, and interpersonal relationships (Murphy and Donovan 1999). Our study was congruent with this general research literature. The major finding of our study is that when meditation is introduced in an academic setting it can have positive long-term effects on both the personal and professional lives of educators. Most of the participants felt that meditation helped them become calmer and more grounded in their life and work.

What I Learned Regarding the Process of Teaching Mediation

Contemplative Practices Can Be Integrated into the Higher Education Curriculum

My experience of introducing contemplative practices to students has been a very positive one. In over twenty years, I have never had a complaint from a student or administrator about asking students to engage in contemplative practice. In fact, my evening and summer classes are always full with a waiting list. The first day of class, I make it very clear that contemplative practices will be an integral part of the course. As I mentioned above, only one student out of two thousand had concerns about meditation – because of her religious background.

My Personal Practice Does Not Have to Be Compartmentalized and Kept Separate from My Professional Work

The line between personal and professional can be a fine one. I have found that I can share my own practice in a manner that supports the student's development. As stated above, a clear rationale for doing this must be provided particularly with reference to teacher education and teacher development. I also find that it is helpful if I share an explanation of why I have engaged in contemplative practices in my own life so that students see the context of the practice in my life (Miller 2008).

Student Ownership of the Practice

I introduce several different types of practice so students can find one that will work for them. As much as possible, I try to make students feel ownership in the practice so some students have modified their practice. For example, one student who swam every day brought mindful awareness to his swimming. Another student during the term had been on vacation and found that sitting on the hotel room balcony and listening to the waves was contemplative; when she returned home, she imagined sitting on the balcony and listening to the waves. Students also monitor the length of time that they meditate. If they find the practice very challenging then I suggest doing it for just five to ten minutes, while other students are more comfortable doing twenty or thirty minutes.

Having Modest Expectations from the Practice

Some students have unreasonable expectations about meditation practice and what it will do for them. I suggest to the students to adopt an approach of inquiry; in other words, try the practice and just keep an open mind about what happens. Treat each session as a unique experience. If the previous session was one where the student felt calm and relaxed, do not carry that expectation to the next session. In fact, each moment of practice should be seen with a here-and-now awareness.

Forget about Doing It Right

Probably the most common concern that beginning students have is "Am I doing it right?" Because contemplative practice can be so foreign in our produce-and-consume culture, students need to let go of judging their practice. The main focus is on simply settling down and developing the awareness. We live in such a performance-oriented culture that students want to know how they are doing. Below is an example of how a student worried about getting it right:

> Looking back at my journal, I remember being plagued by the rush of thoughts that seemed to pour into the void in my mind when I meditated. I felt like I couldn't control or stop what was happening to me. Then panic hit, was I doing "it" right?

Eventually this student shifted her approach:

> In the end I thought I could take one of two paths – give up meditation or stop worrying about doing meditation the right way and just enjoy the half hour that I gave myself as a gift. At this point, I no longer felt the need to control thoughts, just to experience them and be mindful of their presence. Meditation was no longer a struggle or fight for control, but a chance to reflect and be calm.

Another student had an insight that allowed her to let go of her trying to get it "right":

> There were a few frustrating days at this point when I felt like giving up – I was not getting anywhere. But then I decided there was nowhere to get to, no place I had to be!

In our daily lives, we are constantly planning something, doing, and then evaluating what we have done. I suggest to students that in meditation we give up these activities and as much as possible just be.

Let Go of the Story

Shunryu Suzuki Roshi told his students to "welcome the thoughts but just do not serve them tea." Story and narrative have a place in our lives but not in meditation. As much as possible, I encourage students to not

engage the stories that come up during the practice and return to the focus (e.g., breath, mantra, etc.). This is a challenge for even the most experienced meditator so when we do engage the story I suggest letting go of
the judgment.

Celebrate the Awareness

A session may be filled with our stories and concerns but usually there are
moments of awareness. One helpful approach is to celebrate the moment
of awareness when it does arise. Instead of condemning ourselves for being lost in the thoughts, we can rejoice at the moments of awareness no
matter how brief or fleeting.

Connecting to the Body

For many students, the practice allowed them to reconnect with their
bodies. In our culture, and particularly in education, we tend to live in
our heads. Many of the students began to connect more directly to the
physical experience of the body. One student put it this way:

> During the meditation you have no choice but to listen to your body. It en-
> ables you to not only become in touch with your thoughts and emotions, but
> also to realize that everything is connected to your physical body.

What I Learned about the Relationship between
Meditation and Teaching

Patience

We live in a society where we constantly witness impatience. Consider the
roadways that are filled with impatient drivers and the exasperated individuals we see waiting in lineups in the grocery store. We see impatience
in our children who are used to watching television shows and videos
that are geared to the short attention span.

As teachers, we need to cultivate patience. Children learn at different
rates and in different ways. Some students can test our patience in that
they seem to learn slowly, while other students' behaviour in the classroom can challenge our patience. However, if we can be patient and not
be reactive, learning and behaviour can change. Every teacher has had the
experience of a student's behaviour irritating us, but if we do not react in

a negative way there can be positive change. Once, I had a male student who seemed frustrated and unhappy in my class; yet, when I told the class that I would not be teaching next year because of administrative commitments, he stated that he was upset that he could not take my class in the fall. I did not react to his problematic behaviour and found that patience rather than reactivity worked.

Meditation and mindfulness cultivate patience. Sitting quietly for twenty or thirty minutes, we learn to sit with a range of emotions and thoughts without trying to change them. People say that meditation is boring, but learning to sit with and watch the boredom cultivates patience that can be transferred into our teaching.

One of my students in the Initial Teacher Education course identified patience as an outcome of the meditation practice and its place in his life and teaching:

> Patience. My fuse used to be pretty short, but now I have a lot more patience and I deal with things that come up in a different way. I'm no longer angry, when a bunch of people crowd into the elevator and press every floor below mine. Now, I simply enjoy the ride. Patience has also helped me a great deal in relating to the students in my classroom.

The Importance of Attention

Roger Walsh (1999) offers a story to illustrate the importance of attention:

> A student of Zen purchased a spiritual text. Bringing it to the monastery, the student asked if the teacher would write some words of inspiration in it.
> "Certainly," replied the teacher, who wrote for a second then handed the book back. There the student found only a single word: "Attention!"
> "Will you not write more?" pleaded the disappointed student, again offering the book to the teacher.
> "All right," said the teacher, who this time wrote for several seconds. Inside the book the student now found three words:
> Attention! Attention! Attention! (150)

Ken McLeod (2002) identifies three stages in the development of attention. The first stage is formal practice, which includes meditation. Meditation practice almost always starts with focusing the attention on some object such as the breath, a sound, or an image. The next stage is extending the attention into daily life. This usually starts with simple activities such as walking, washing the dishes, or folding the laundry. This application of attention of daily life is also called mindfulness. The third and final stage that McLeod describes is living in attention. Here attention is no longer just a practice but an ongoing reality in our everyday lives. It is something that then can arise naturally in our life and work and is often the outcome of many years of meditation and mindfulness practice.

Sustained practice can let teachers be more attentive to their students and, hopefully, it becomes an ongoing reality in the classroom. Some of teachers in my class have commented on how the mindfulness and meditation practice transferred to the classroom and how it made teaching more enjoyable. For example, one teacher from Japan wrote:

> Being mindful in our classrooms we are able to slow our thoughts and actions and become aware of our students' needs, see how we are meeting them, and how the students are affected and respond to our actions ... When we teach mindfully we know what we are teaching. We are aware of the words we speak, the tone in which we speak them, we are able to deeply observe and listen to our students and are aware of connectedness between student and teacher and indeed all the members of the classroom community. We are able to see the presentation of the curriculum and adjust it to the situation.

For teachers, there are important behaviors to be mindfully considered: body language, eye contact and compassionate speech. As I walk down the hall from my office where I have been handling administrative duties to my classroom where I want to shift my focus to my students, I try to pay attention to my walk – my posture, my speed, my gait. I relax the muscles in my face and put on a smile. Sometimes that smile comes more naturally than at other times but the result is always the same – my mood shifts and I become less defensive and more receptive. I start each class with erect posture, looking forward and ready to meet the students. I think my body language has a strong positive impact on the start of each class.

Eye contact is an extension of body language and a very real and immediate way to focus on the students. I try to make eye contact with every student as I walk through the class. They are usually engaged in a variety of activities and conversations but my eye contact and my close physical proximity to each student allow them to refocus on our class and we connect with each other.

Presence

Attention allows the teacher to be more present to the individual student. Below is how one elementary school teacher became more attentive to the needs of an individual student and the difference she felt this made. This student (ZR) had been acting out a great deal in the classroom:

> Today ZR and I spoke briefly about his difficulty to focus. Today was particularly difficult for him. He did try very hard. As other students responded during our math discussion, he wiggled and wiggled in his seat. In the past, I had been frustrated with him – his distractions became the class's distractions. Today, I was mindful. I only thought of him in that moment.
>
> I felt a great deal of empathy for him. I remembered how difficult it had been (and sometimes still is) for me to sit still in class. He looked at me watching him with what seemed like a slightly guilty look. I smiled at him and he smiled back and seemed to be trying even harder to sit still, to focus.
>
> After the discussion was over and the students worked on their project, I went over to talk with him. (He has chosen to sit by himself at a desk right next to mine.) We had a good talk. I listened, he talked. Eventually, he suggested taking breaks between his work. He promised to work hard. I said we could try it for few days and then bring the suggestion to his parents as he also expressed concern about difficulties focusing during his homework.

Later, this teacher and ZR met with his parents:

> ZR and I had a meeting with his parents after school today. We presented them with a simple "schedule" for his day – 10 minutes of work followed by a 10-minute break. I sensed by his mother's response that she was quite taken aback. This was school and he should be able to focus. His sister did her homework without any breaks. ZR explained, as much as he could, how and why he was having difficulty and why he felt the 10-minute breaks might help. He promised to work very hard during the 10-minute workouts. Because he had actually been experimenting, I could vouch that he had been working very hard and producing excellent work.
>
> I think this meeting was the first that I have had in a long time where I felt that I was there. I wasn't worried about getting home. I wasn't concerned about what they would think of me as a teacher. My own experience with a "cluttered mind" made me believe that for ZR to be "here" and present, he needed breaks to immerse himself in his art. I felt comfortable. We'll monitor this strategy until the Christmas break and revisit in January.

In the day when drugs are administered to children so they can settle down, this example shows how this teacher's presence made a difference in this student's life.

Compassion

Another outcome that some teachers have identified is greater compassion for their students. This usually arises from those students who have practised the loving-kindness meditation. But even being mindful and slowing down can lead to the rise of compassion. One teacher made the connection being mindfulness and compassion:

> For me love or compassion for my students has become a central priority in my classroom. Compassion comes from the ability to focus on a student – to listen deeply to their words, empathize with their situation and care about the outcome ... A teacher who can focus on each student is more likely to act compassionately, thus creating a true receiving of others.
>
> An increased effort to speak more compassionately comes out of being more mindful. When I reflect on my spoken words, I am amazed by all of the things I say without deliberate consideration. I dismiss people's ideas, judge and criticize their words and actions, and fail to listen deeply to their feelings when I quickly, curtly and sternly utter my comments. I have tried over the years to speak with more compassion. This more attentive way to speak in turn slows my speaking down and allows me to be more compassionate – more of an active listener who is truly responding to students' actions and words.

What I Learned about the Transformational Nature of Meditation Practice

Some students in my class reported that meditation had a transformational impact on their lives. Often, this was characterized as a powerful sense of interconnectedness to others, the environment, and the universe. One teacher wrote this:

> "Connectedness" is what we all crave, really! Through meditation, I have been able to re-connect with the life within me. I know that continued practice will enable me to replenish my soul so that what once was the "drain" of teaching will become life-giving. (Also, we can find life within our students with which we can also connect!)

Another student commented on the mysterious nature of the process:

I found meditation was truly mysterious. At times I would have insights or experiences, which could not be explained. "Where did that insight emerge from?" Oftentimes I felt in these situations (these rare situations) I tapped something greater than me. I felt a connection to something greater. This did not feel like a religious connection ... rather a connection to the universe.

I also found a certain degree of reverence for the process. It is not something you can "make happen" – it happens to you. I couldn't help feeling many times that something else, something mysterious was at play.

Another student wrote:

It is in these moments of complete focus that I have frequently experienced a oneness with a Higher Power. I rejoice in these moments of total oneness.

A student from China who had lived through the Cultural Revolution found the process allowed him to connect to humanity:

In our meditation practice I have found so much in common to share with others, making me feel that human beings, be they Westerners or Orientals, are in one way or another connected in our inner world. Once this common point is explored, there would be opportunity for us to improve the quality of our lives ... We may gain a better understanding of what we are doing, we see more connections with the rest of the world.

One woman who worked as a counsellor for survivors of incest, sexual abuse, and partner assault wrote of the impact of meditation in an almost poetic manner:

Through meditation I feel that I am being gently invited to observe the nature of my own humanity. Personally I had been strongly moved and transformed through the beautiful nature of this spiritual practice. I had heard my voice and soul with amusement. I had slowly let my inner judge go away and be more in touch with the unspoken, the unseen, and the sacred part of myself. I had achieved a larger vision of my self and my reality, a vision that tenderly dilutes my fears, preconceptions, judgments and need for control. Because of meditation I had been able to transform my fear, anger, and resistance into joy, forgiveness, acceptance and love.

I can bring to meditation anything that is for the purpose of seeing it or feeling it. The reflection and contemplation offered by this practice provides a very safe and comfortable environment where my creativity, intuition, and imagination can be enlarged. I can feel, see, and reflect on my reality while I confess my own fears and personal dilemmas to the being that exists within myself. I become my own witness, my own mentor, and my own source of liberation. I can unveil the many layers that cover my real nature so I can then be able to recognize my own needs and inclinations.

Meditating has also been a road of discovering for me. I first discovered the honouring power that the soul possesses for every human being. Through meditation I discovered the unconditional acceptance that is available to the heart of every human being. It is through the practice of meditation that I had better understood the meaning and importance of accepting and honoring myself and others.

Transformation can lead to how the teacher sees her students. Below are the insights of a teacher who had been doing walking meditation as her practice. She sees herself and her students as "one growing, changing organism":

However, my thinking is expanding somewhat to stretch into a new sense of what it means to know someone, student or colleague, in a way that facilitates true and effective learning and growth. To teach from an intuitive source is to submit myself to an ocean of largeness of possibility that roars and flows with its own greatness and power quite outside the realm of my orchestration and planning and timing. It is to let go of the illusion of my own control and expertness, recognizing instead that to limit my students to the meager feelings of my ego is to miss the hugeness and importance of authentic educative growth. I am reminded here of my earlier teaching days, furiously pouring over the little section on China in the Social Studies binder, pathetically planning what glorious reams of knowledge I might impart, only to realize with horror that two-thirds of my class were *born* there. Who do I think I am? Teaching from the ego is ultimately a crash-course in humiliation. It is only when I submit to the truth of my smallness as one who is learning and struggling along a humble growth road with these brothers and sisters who are my students that I come closest to teaching in truth.

... so crucial and authentic was the experience of "teaching through living" with my students, that I have since found myself questioning the validity of some of my former practice. I am beginning to see my students and myself as ultimately one growing, changing organism continuing to become. I am only beginning this journey; there is so much that is new and unknown to me about the scope and breadth of holistic teaching and living. I only know that it is becoming my passion and perhaps my life-work to teach and to live from the fireside, to "be quiet and listen and see what we hear."

This teacher shows insight, humility, and love in this passage. For example, she realizes that many of her students probably have more knowledge of China than she does since they were born there. She has the insight that she cannot *control* the educational experiences of her students. Finally, she feels love for her students as she sees "my students and myself as ultimately one growing, changing organism continuing to become." I am convinced that wisdom can come from teachers working on themselves through various mind-and-body practices. These practices allow teachers to move from just teaching from their head to teaching with their whole being. From this wholeness, wisdom can arise in our schools and classrooms.

Conclusion

It is my belief that contemplative practices both ground the student and, at the same time, provide a basic energy to my courses. Focusing on the flow of the breath is a method most often selected by my students in choosing a meditative practice. Breathing is a basic life function, and our awareness of breathing brings us into the here-and-now. Breathing is a natural and organic process that can ground our experience. Like life itself, each breath can bring us into the present moment. Besides grounding the students, there is the rhythm of breathing. I have argued that also in teaching we need rhythm, otherwise the classroom becomes too static (Miller 2011). Waldorf education has used the metaphor of breathing to demonstrate how there should be movement in the classroom. The breath, then, can be seen as symbolic of the flow of energy in the classroom. Finally, there is also mystery around the breath. The word "spiritual" finds its roots in the Latin, *spiritus*, which means breath. There is the space between the out breath and the in breath, a place of "in between." Ferrer (2002), in his book on transpersonal theory, refers to the work of Buber and the "Between." In Buber's (1970) words, "Spirit is not in the I but between I and you, it is not like the blood that circulates in you, but like the air you breathe" (89). Ferrer argues that the Between is the "locus of genuine spiritual realization" (119). Awareness of both the flow and spaces in breathing can provide a place for soul to come forth.

Much discourse in higher education is dominated by critical theory, and Nel Noddings (2003) has identified a problem with this focus:

> A great worry for critical theorists – one that should receive far more attention than it does at present – is that efforts of critical pedagogues induce anger, alienation, and hopelessness instead of wisdom and practical action. "Discussion" can deteriorate into venting and blaming thus causing increased separation among groups. (104)

There is a place for critical theory in higher education but contemplative education also needs to be in the curriculum. Contemplative practices nurture awareness and holistic experience. Contemplative practices provide students with experiences that are life affirming and potentially liberating. Again, the student's comments cited above are worth repeating here: "I become my own witness, my own mentor and my own source of liberation." The experience of soul arose through the practice:

> Meditating has also been a road of discovering for me. I first discovered the honoring power that the soul possesses for every human being.

As I write this, I have just completed two sections of my course on Holistic Education where forty-eight students were engaged in meditation practice throughout the course. Reading the students' reflections on their practice, I was often moved by their comments. One student wrote:

> To my surprise feeling grew into *being* from the inside, which precipitated a sense of connectivity with the world. It was as though ... I was lit up from the inside out.

Ultimately, I believe contemplative practice is about bringing out the light within each of us. My experience in working with contemplative practices continues to inspire and deeply nourish my own soul.

Jack's Journey

In education, as in other areas, there is a lot of emphasis on story. People are being encouraged to tell their stories as a way of interpreting or framing their own experiences. In my classes at OISE, I tell my own story. I do it in the spirit of Emerson (2003), when he wrote about a preacher but we can substitute teacher:

> He ... had lived in vain. He had not one word intimating that he had laughed, or wept, was married or in love had been commended or cheated, or chagrined. If he had ever lived and acted we were none the wiser for it. (257)

I find that students welcome the opportunity to hear about my own journey so I am closing the book with my own story.

I was born in 1943 and raised in Kansas City, Missouri, where my parents provided a loving and secure environment. My mother's name, Joy, was so appropriate as she had a wonderful sense of humour. She could make me and others in her life laugh. I can remember many times in my childhood sharing a smile, giggle, or a laugh with her. My father, who seemed remote in my childhood, became a more important figure in my life during adolescence and young adulthood. We both liked sports, and we would talk a lot about baseball and particularly football at the University of Missouri where both my mother and father went to school. My father respected my right to make my own decisions even though some of my choices were not those that he would have made. My Dad's name was John and I was also given the name John. However, I was soon given the nickname "Jack" by my parents. My grandmother, Faith, was the other significant adult in my life. She introduced me to the wonder of music by giving me Beethoven's 5th Symphony when I was in Grade 6, and to this day I have found a spiritual connection to music, particularly the work of Mozart, Bach, and Haydn. My grandmother also introduced me to Tolstoy's spiritual writing when I was in high school. I had good friends growing up but I also remember spending a lot of time by myself as I particularly liked to read.

I have an older brother, Bill. Over the years, we have grown closer. As I write this, he has just taken on a faculty position at the University of Missouri School of Medicine. Since we both attended the University of Missouri, in Columbia, we follow their football and basketball teams every year.

I attended the University of Missouri for my B.A. and then went to Harvard in 1965 to pursue a Master of Arts in Teaching. It was in Boston that I met my first wife, Jean, whom I married in December 1967. Jean came from a Boston Irish background that was so different from my

Midwestern background; yet, it was clear from the beginning that we were meant to be together.

Jean and I began our married life in the Midwest as I worked at Grinnell College, in Iowa, and the University of Missouri at Kansas City (UMKC). Our first married year was that turbulent year of 1968. Like so many Americans, I still remember vividly where we were when Martin Luther King and Bobby Kennedy were shot. I also recall August when we were moving to Kansas City where I would begin a job teaching at the University of Missouri at Kansas City. The Russians had invaded Czechoslovakia and when we were settling in our new apartment in Kansas City, we watched the riots at the Democratic Convention in Chicago on television. The debates between Gore Vidal and William Buckley, I felt, characterized the deep divisions of that time.

That year of 1968 I began my spiritual search. I had been raised a Christian (Disciples of Christ), but as I confronted the draft and the Vietnam War, I needed something more to deal with the anxiety I was feeling. I had filed a Conscientious Objector statement that was not pacifist, but directed against US intervention in Vietnam. I quoted Thoreau (1983) in my statement:

> It is not a man's duty as a matter of course, to devote himself to the eradication of any, even the most enormous wrong; he may still properly have other concerns to engage him; but it is his duty, at least to wash his hands of it ... If the injustice is part of the necessary friction of the machine of government, let it go ... but if it is of such nature that it requires you to be the agent of injustice to another, then I say, break the law. (396)

Thoreau and Emerson have been two of my teachers throughout my life (Miller 2011). Since I believed that the US intervention was wrong, I was prepared to resist the draft and thus break the law. Jean and I had decided that if I was inducted, we would go to Canada. The possibility of such a change in my life created a tremendous amount of stress. I suffered from dizzy spells and nervous tension. The stress began to interfere with my work at UMKC, so I began to look for ways to deal with my problems. Sometime during the fall of 1968, I read Jess Stearn's *Yoga, Youth and Reincarnation*, which described some simple hatha yoga exercises that I began to practice every day. Within weeks, I began to feel more relaxed. In short, the draft started me on my spiritual journey. I became interested in the spiritual framework that underpinned the yoga, and I began reading about Eastern spiritual practices.

I received my induction notice in April of 1969, and Jean and I began to make our plans to go to Canada. We emigrated to Toronto in June of that year, and I began my doctoral studies in education at the Ontario Institute of Studies in Education at the University of Toronto. The pain of leaving my parents that June morning in 1969 is still vivid in my memory as I can still see them standing sadly at the door as Jean and I drove away. When we arrived Toronto the next day, we found that our furniture hadn't arrived at our apartment so Jean and I bought air mattresses and army blankets so we could sleep in our frigid apartment. That summer I alternated between exhilaration and depression as I felt "at home" in Canada, yet I often became depressed at the thought that I might never again be able to travel to the United States to see my family. In a sense, going to Canada was like a death, because I had to let go of so much.

Eventually, we settled into life in Toronto. Our first child, Patrick, was born there in 1970. When I graduated, I took a job in Thunder Bay, Ontario, working with the Ontario Institute for Studies in Education in their field office. My work involved working with schools in a consultant's capacity. Thunder Bay is located two hundred miles north of Duluth, Minnesota, and is relatively isolated. Snow settles on the ground in November and doesn't leave until the beginning of April.

Helping me through these difficult years of change was my wife, Jean. Her warmth and love provided the support that carried me through these transitions. We both began to see our marriage as a spiritual partnership or a mutual environment for our spiritual growth. Jean also did the yoga, and we both shared an interest in Eastern spirituality. The teachings of Ram Dass were helpful to us, and I can still remember us falling to sleep at night listening to his words on tape. We both began to see that our lives had a meaning and purpose and that we were connected to something much larger than ourselves. It was through the Ram Dass literature that I was introduced to the work of Goldstein and Kornfield. In 1974, I ordered a set of tapes of Joseph Goldstein on meditation instruction. These tapes provided the beginning of my own meditation practice, which I have continued to this day.

In 1976 Jean's father died, and in 1977 my mother passed away. The work of Elizabeth Kubler-Ross was very helpful to Jean and me and gave us a framework for understanding and working with the painfulness of these losses. She helped us see death as another transition, rather than as the end. At the same time, joy came with the birth of our daughter, Nancy, in 1976.

The year 1982 was another watershed year for Jean and myself. I attended my first meditation retreat at Barre, Massachusetts, which was conducted by Jack Kornfield and Sharon Salzburg. The retreat was two weeks long and consisted of alternating sitting and walking meditation throughout the day. Much of the retreat was spent sitting in pain as my knees and legs ached. However, halfway through the retreat I felt a sense of joy and rapture that permeated my whole being. The two weeks helped me deepen my practice.

Shortly after Christmas that year, Jean told me she had a lump in her breast. I couldn't believe that she might have cancer. I remember that time as one when she went for tests and I read as much as possible about the disease. We got a call one Sunday morning in January to say she should come in that day for her surgery that would take place the next day. Oh, how low I felt as I drove her to the hospital. After the operation Jean lay in the room, and I sat with her as I waited for her to awaken. As I looked at her, I felt such compassion and the deep realization that we were connected beyond time and space. Up until this point, we had had a wonderful marriage based on love and trust, but now we started on a journey that resulted in spiritual union.

Jean recovered rapidly from the surgery and her usual buoyant spirits returned. I remember her swinging her arm around two days after the surgery to show me how good she felt. The prognosis, however, wasn't good since the cancer had spread to the lymph nodes. She had to have chemotherapy, and the treatments became increasingly more difficult as she lost her hair and she was nauseous after each treatment. However, at the end of the treatments she bounced back. The work of Bernie Siegel was very helpful to Jean as she began her fight with cancer.

At this time, we moved to St Catharines, in southern Ontario, where Jean loved her new home and surroundings. She reached out to make new friends, and she completed her honours degree in psychology at Brock University. There was no evidence of any recurrence of the cancer for almost three years.

In September of 1986, however, we began our final journey together. I knew something was wrong when she had trouble remembering simple words. One morning, I was going out shopping, and she couldn't remember the word "muffin" and I cried out to her, "What's happening?" In a couple of weeks, her memory got worse and we rushed to the doctor's. He ordered an emergency CAT scan. We learned in a few days that the cancer had spread to the brain and that Jean had to undergo radiation treatment for two weeks. For several weeks, Jean could hardly express herself and I had to be with her constantly. However, worse was to come as she became very weak from the treatments and she lay sleeping on the couch except to get up for meals. She slept almost around the clock for six weeks; her legs became very thin. Around Christmas, she began to recover as she gained energy and her memory improved. In January, it looked like she might fully recover when we received more devastating news – the cancer had spread to her lung. She now began a new round of chemotherapy treatments. Jean handled these treatments very well and began to return to a normal lifestyle. The cancer was in remission. We were able to travel to Florida in March of 1987, and she was horseback riding in late April. People marvelled at her spirits and at how she recovered. Jean had hardly been able to walk in December, and in April she was living a normal life and horseback riding even while she was still taking the chemotherapy treatments.

The real miracle, however, was that there was a spiritual awakening that paralleled her awakening from her long rest in November and December. The last year of her life, Jean lived in Christ consciousness. Despite the pain and fear, her eyes radiated a warmth and glow that came from her spiritual heart. She was totally centred in a way that she had never been until she became sick. I remember her saying so often even in the midst of her cancer – "I feel so blessed." Throughout our marriage, Jean said that I was her teacher, but in the last year of her life she became my teacher. I marvelled at her courage and spiritual presence. The cancer made me surrender completely to what was happening. Meditation practice proved invaluable as in the practice you have to witness pain in your body. By accepting pain in ourselves we learn to be present to pain in others.

We got more bad news that fall when we learned that the cancer had spread to the liver. She was treated again with chemotherapy. Again, Jean seemed to sail through the treatments, and we spent a wonderful Christmas together that year. We went to Florida with the kids in March and as Jean walked the beach, she remarked, "This is heaven." Jean always loved the ocean and was most joyful and peaceful when she was near the water. I couldn't have dreamed then that she would die in a few weeks. Jean's approach to life at that time was like the Zen story of the man who was hanging from a cliff facing certain death below when his grip finally tired. Despite the presence of death, the man reached out to take a strawberry growing on the cliffside and savoured each bite as he ate it. Jean, who knew that she was going to die, savoured each moment with her family whom she loved so deeply.

Jean died at home, on 11 April 1988, where she wanted to be. She needed only Tylenol those last days. Despite the cancer, she always felt blessed because of her family and the love that they returned to her. A few minutes after Jean died, Patrick, our son, came into the room and hugged his mother. I sat with Jean that evening and waited for the doctor to come to pronounce her dead. I read passages from Stephen Levine's book that help a soul move into the light. When the undertaker came, Nancy, our daughter, and Patrick picked out an outfit for their mother. I was amazed at the strength and calmness they showed in the presence of death.

It was through Jean that I learned about the fundamentals of life – suf-· fering, love, and death. It was through this experience that the teaching of the Buddha and Christ came alive. However, in the end, it was clear that my wife, Jean, had become my most powerful and wisest teacher. Our marriage could be viewed as a spiritual partnership where we helped each other through our respective crises so that we could touch the oneness.

Since Jean's death, I have been married twice. Both of these women have also been my teachers. Susan Drake, a professor at Brock University, taught me about the importance of taking care of my body. Up until I met Susan, I never exercised but my walks with her showed how I needed to respect the body. We also worked together on various books and articles in holistic education. Finally, she helped me navigate the difficult years after Jean's death. Recently, my daughter learned that she had breast cancer. Susan was very much saddened by this news and has continued to share her concern and support for my daughter during this difficult time.

Both my children are very dear to me. Patrick is a professor in philosophy at Duquesne University in Pittsburg, and his wife, Sarah, has given birth to my two grandchildren, Simon and Mary Jean. My son and I share a passionate interest in baseball. Nancy has taught ESL and is a serous practitioner of yoga and is now taking a one-year dance program at the Laban School in London.

I am now married to Midori Sakurai whom I met in Japan when I was giving talks there in 1994. Midori is a healing presence in my life and to my children and grandchildren. She travelled to London to be with my daughter when she had her operation for breast cancer and travelled to Pittsburgh to help my son's family shortly after both their children were born. I usually go to Japan every year to teach a course in Holistic Education at Kobe Shinwa Women's University and Midori translates for me. We enjoy working together there. Midori also makes beautiful objects out of wool through felting (http://midostail-felt.blogspot.ca). She has been my teacher as well, and one of the many things she has taught me is to appreciate animals. I already mentioned in the last chapter how she has taught me the importance of gratitude.

When this book is published, I will be seventy years old. I am still teaching full time and continue to draw inspiration from the students I work with. I am very grateful that I have been able to introduce contemplative practices to my students and also supervise several doctoral theses on contemplative education. Teaching and working with young people continue to bring much joy into my life. I see no reason to retire as long as this is true.

Bibliography

Allen, Gay W. 1981. *Waldo Emerson*. New York: Viking.

Armstrong, Karen. 2006. *The Great Transformation: The Beginning of Our Religious Traditions*. New York: Alfred Knopf.

Armstrong, Karen. 2011. *Twelve Steps to a Compassionate Life*. New York: Alfred Knopf.

Armstrong, Karen. 2012 *Charter for Compassion*. http://charterforcompassion.org

Aurelius, Marcus. 1997. *Meditations*. Mineola, NY: Dover.

Bache, Christopher M. 2008. *The Living Classroom: Teaching and Collective Consciousness*. Albany, NY: SUNY Press.

Bancroft, Anne. 1982. *The Luminous Vision: Six Medieval Mystics and Their Teachings*. London: Unwin.

Benson, Herbert. 1976. *The Relaxation Response*. New York: Harper Torch Books.

Bernstein, Robert J. 1976. *The Restructuring of Social and Political Theory*. New York: Harcourt Brace Jovanovich.

Bodian, S. 1985. The heart of prayer: An interview with Christian contemplative David Steindl-Rast. *Yoga Journal* 1985 (May/June): 25–8.

Bohm, David. 1980. *Wholeness and the Implicate Order*. London: Routledge and Kegan Paul.

Bohm, David, and R. Weber. 1982. Nature as creativity. *ReVision*, 5, no. 2: 35–40.

Bolton, Gillie. 2010. *Reflective Practice*. Thousand Oaks, CA: Sage.

Boyce, Barry. 2011. Creating a mindful society. In *The Mindfulness Revolution*, ed. Barry Boyce, 252–64. Boston: Shambhala.

Broad, William. 2012. *The Science of Yoga: The Risks and the Rewards*. New York: Simon and Schuster.

Brown, Joseph E. 1989. *The Sacred Pipe: Black Elk's Account of the Seven Rites of the Oglala Sioux*. Norman, OK: University of Oklahoma Press.

Buber, Martin. 1970. *I and Thou*. Trans. W. Kaufman. New York: Scribner.

Buchmann, Margret. 1989. The careful vision: How practical is contemplation in teaching? *American Journal of Education* 98 (1): 35–61. http://dx.doi.org/10.1086/443943

Bush, Mirabai. 2011. Contemplative higher education in contemplative life. In *Contemplative Nation: How Ancient Practices Are Changing the Way We Live*, ed. Mirabai Bush, 221–36. Kalamazoo, MI: Fetzer Institute.

Cameron, Silver Donald. 29 Dec. 2009. Interview with Prime Minister of Bhutan. *Chronicle Herald*. http://thechronicleherald.ca/NovaScotian/1159562.html

Campbell, Joseph. 1949. *The Hero with a Thousand Faces*. Princeton, NJ: Princeton University Press.

Capaldi, Nicolas, Eugene Kelly, and Luis E. Navia. 1981. *Introduction to Philosophy*. Amherst, NY: Prometheus Books.

Capps, Walter Holden, ed. 1976. *Seeing with a Native Eye: Essays on Native American Religion*. New York: Harper Forum Books.

Carrington, Patricia. 1977. *Freedom in Meditation*. Garden City, NY: Anchor Books/Doubleday.

Center for Contemplative Mind in Society. 2012. Mission Statement for the Association of Contemplative Mind in Higher Education. http://www.contemplativemind.org/programs/acmhe

Chadwick, David. 1999. *Crooked Cucumber: The Life and Zen Teachings of Shunryu Suzuki*. New York: Broadway Books.

Cohen, Avraham. 2009. *Gateway to the Dao-Field: Essays for the Awakening Educator*. Amherst, NY: Cambria Press.

Cousins, Norman. 2005. *Anatomy of an Illness: As Perceived by the Patient*. New York: Norton.

Csikszentmihalyi, Mihaly. 1988. The flow experience and human psychology. In *Optimal Experience: Psychological Studies in Flow in Consciousness*, eds. M. Csikszentmihalyi and I.S. Csikszentmihalyi, 364–83. Cambridge: Cambridge University Press. http://dx.doi.org/10.1017/CBO9780511621956.002.

Csikszentmihalyi, Mihaly, and I.S. Csikszentmihalyi, eds. 1988. *Optimal Experience: Psychological Studies of Flow in Consciousness*. Cambridge: Cambridge University Press. http://dx.doi.org/10.1017/CBO9780511621956.

Dante Alighieri. 1984. *Paradiso: The Third Book of the Divine Comedy*. A. New York: Quality Paperback Book Club.

Dass, Ram, and Paul Gorman. 1985. *How Can I Help? Stories and Reflections on Service*. New York: Alfred Knopf.

Davidson, Richard J., with Sharon Begley. 2012. *The Emotional Life of Your Brain*. New York: Hudson Street Press.

de Nicolás, Antonio, ed. 1989. *Habits of Mind: An Introduction to the Philosophy of Education*. New York: Paragon.

DeMaille, Raymond J. 1984. *The Sixth Grandfather: Black Elk's Teachings Given to John G. Neihardt*. Lincoln, NE: University of Nebraska Press.

DeMaille, Raymond J. 2008. John G. Neihardt and Nicholas Black Elk. In John Neihardt, *Black Elk Speaks*, 289–316. Albany, NY: SUNY Press.

Deshimaru, Taisen. 1985. *Questions to a Zen Master: Political and Spiritual Answers from the Great Japanese Master*. New York: Dutton.

Easwaran, Eknath. 1977. *The Mantram Handbook: Formulas for Transformation*. Berkeley, CA: Nilgiri Press.

Easwaran, Eknath. 1978. *Gandhi the Man*. Berkeley, CA: Nilgiri Press.

Einstein, Albert. 1984. *Einstein: A Portrait*. Corte Madera, CA: Pomegranate Artbooks.

Eisner, Elliot, and Elizabeth Vallance, eds. 1974. *Conflicting Conceptions of Curriculum*. Berkeley, CA: McCutchan.

Emerson, Ralph Waldo. 1909–14. *The Journals of Ralph Waldo Emerson*. Eds. Edward Emerson and Waldo Emerson Forbes. Vol. IX. Boston: Houghton Mifflin.

Emerson, Ralph Waldo. 2003. *Selected Writings*. New York: Signet Classics.

Erdman, Jean. 1987. Reflecting on teaching and adult education. *Lifelong Learning* 10 (8): 19–22.

Feinstein, David, and Stanley Krippner. 1988. *Personal Mythology: The Psychology of Your Evolving Self*. Los Angeles, CA: Tarcher.

Ferrer, Jorge N. 2002. *Revisioning Transpersonal Theory: A Participatory Vision of Human Spirituality*. Albany, NY: SUNY Press.

Fischer, Louis. 1954. *Gandhi: His Life and Message for the World*. New York: Mentor.

Fischer, Norman. 2011. Mindfulness for everyone. In *The Mindfulness Revolution*, ed. Barry Boyce, 49–56. Boston: Shambhala.

Flinders, Carol L. 1993. *Enduring Grace: Living Portraits of Seven Women Mystics*. San Francisco: HarperSanFrancisco.

Forbes, David. 2004. *Boyz 2 Buddhas: Counseling Urban High School Male Athletes in the Zone*. New York: Peter Lang.

Freedman, Samuel G. 1990. *Small Victories: The Real World of a Teacher, Her Students and Their High School*. New York: Harper and Row.

Furlong, Monica. 1980. *Merton: A Biography*. New York: Harper.

Gandhi, Mohandas K. 1999. *The Way to God*. Berkeley, CA: Berkeley Hills.

Garrison Institute. CARE program. 2012. http://www.garrisoninstitute.org/
  contemplation-and-education/care-for-teachers

Goldstein, Joseph. 1976. *The Experience of Insight: A Natural Unfolding*. Santa
  Cruz, CA: Unity Press.

Goldstein, Joseph, and Jack Kornfield. 1987. *Seeking the Heart of Wisdom: The
  Path of Insight Meditation*. Boston: Shambhala.

Green, Shawn. 2011. *The Way of Baseball: Finding Stillness at 95 mph*.
  New York: Simon and Schuster.

Greenwood, Ernest. 1966. Attributes of a profession. In *Professionalization*, eds.
  Howard Vollmer and Donald Mills, 10–19. Englewood Cliffs, NJ: Prentice
  Hall.

Griffin, Robert. 1977, Feb. Discipline: What's it taking out of you? *Learning*,
  77–80.

Hadot, Pierre. 2002. *What Is Ancient Philosophy?* Cambridge, MA: Harvard
  University Press.

Hall, Debbie. 2007. I Believe in Presence. In *This I Believe: The Personal
  Philosophies of Remarkable Men and Women*, eds. Jay Allison and Dan
  Gediman. New York: Henry Holt.100-102

Hanh, Thich Nhat. 1976. *The Miracle of Mindfulness! A Manual on Meditation*.
  Boston: Beacon.

Hanh, Thich Nhat. 1991. *Peace Is Every Step: The Path of Mindfulness in
  Everyday Life*. New York: Bantam.

Hart, William. 1987. *The Art of Living: Vipassana Meditation as Taught by
  S.N. Goenka*. New York: HarperOne.

Harvey, Andrew. 1994. *The Way of Passion: A Celebration of Rumi*. Berkeley,
  CA: Frog.

Hawken, Paul. 2007. *Blessed Unrest: How the Largest Movement in the World
  Came into Being and Why No One Saw It Coming*. New York: Viking.

Hawn Foundation. 2012. MindUP Program. http:// www.thehawnfoundation
  .org/mindup

Hite, Lewis F. 1988. Love: The ultimate reality. In *Emanuel Swedenborg:
  A Continuing Vision*, eds. Robin Larsen, Stephen Larsen, James Lawrence,
  and William Woofenden. New York: Swedenborg Foundation.

Holmes, Oliver Wendell. [1885] 1980. *Ralph Waldo Emerson*. Boston:
  Houghton Mifflin.

Honore, Carl. 2004. *In Praise of Slowness: How a Worldwide Movement Is
  Challenging the Cult of Speed*. San Francisco: HarperSanFrancisco.

Hutcherson, Cendri A., Emma M. Seppala, and James J. Gross. 2008.
  Loving-kindness-meditation increases social connectedness. *Emotion* 8 (5):
  720–24.

Inayat-Khan, Zia. 2011. Islamic and Islamicate contemplative practice in the United States. In *Contemplative Nation: How Ancient Ways Are Changing the Way We Live*, ed. Mirabai Bush. Kalamazoo, MI: Fetzer Institute. 97-108.

Jackson, Phil. 1995. *Sacred Hoops: Spiritual Lessons of a Hardwood Warrior.* New York: Hyperion.

James, William. 2002. *The Varieties of Religious Experience.* New York: Modern Library.

Jennings, Patricia, and David I. Rome. 2011. Envisioning the future of K-12 contemplative education. In *Contemplative Nation: How Ancient Practices Are Changing the Way We Live*, ed. Mirabai Bush, 247–58. Kalamazoo, MI: Fetzer Institute.

Jennings, Patricia, Karin Snowberg, Michael Coccia, and Mark T. Greenberg. 2012. Refinement and evaluation of cultivating awareness and resilience in education for teacher education programs. Paper presented at the Annual Conference of the American Education Research Association, Vancouver, BC.

Johnson, Charles. 2003. Introduction. *Selected Writings of Ralph Waldo Emerson*, vii–xvii. New York: Signet Classics.

Jung, Carl. 1981. *Memories, Dreams, Reflections.* Ed. A. Jaffe. New York: Random House.

Kabat-Zinn, Jon. 1990. *Full Catastrophe Living: Using the Wisdom of Your Body and Mind to Face Stress, Pain, and Illness.* New York: Delacorte.

Kabat-Zinn, Jon. 2005. *Coming to Our Senses: Healing Ourselves and the World through Mindfulness.* New York: Hyperion.

Karmiris, Maria. 2012. Teaching with Heart: Recalling Connections of Loving Kindness. Unpublished ms.

Keller, Helen. 2000. *Light in My Darkness.* West Chester, PA: Chrysalis Books.

Kelley, Kevin W., ed. 1988. *The Home Planet.* Reading, MA: Addison-Wesley.

Knudtson, Pete, and David Suzuki. 1992. *Wisdom of the Elders.* Toronto: Stoddart.

Kornfield, Jack. 1993. *A Path with Heart.* New York: Bantam.

Krishnamurti, Jiddu. 1963. *Life Ahead.* Wheaton, IL: Theosophical Publishing House.

Krishnamurti, Jiddu. 1969. *Freedom from the Known.* New York: Harper and Row.

Kurtz, Ernest, and Katherine Ketcham. 1992. *The Spirituality of Imperfection: Storytelling and the Journey of Wholeness.* New York: Bantam.

Lantieri, Linda. 2012. The Inner Resilience Program. http://www.lindalantieri.org/links_irp.htm

Lao-tsu. 1988. *Tao Te Ching.* Trans. Stephen Mitchell. New York: HarperCollins.

Larsen, Robin, Stephen Larsen, James Lawrence, and William R. Woofenden, eds. 1988. *Emanuel Swedenborg: The Continuing Vision*. New York: Swedenborg Foundation.

Laslo, Ervin. 2009. *Worldshift 2012: Making Green Business, New Politics and Higher Consciousness Work Together*. Toronto: McArthur.

Lerner, Michael. 2000. *Spirit Matters*. Charlottesville, VA: Hampton Roads Publishing.

LeShan, Lawrence. 1974. *How to Meditate: A Guide to Self-Discovery*. Boston: Little, Brown.

Lewis, Franklin D. 2008. *Rumi: Past and Present, East and West*. Oxford: Oneworld Press.

Lewis, Harry R. 2006. *Excellence without a Soul: Does Liberal Education Have a Future?* New York: Public Affairs.

Long, Jeffrey, with Paul Perry. 2010. *Evidence of the Afterlife: The Science of Near Death Experiences*. New York: HarperOne.

Luke, Helen. 1989. *Dark Wood to White Rose*. New York: Parabola.

Lusseryan, Jacques. 1987. *And There Was Light*. New York: Parabola.

Macrorie, K. 1984. *20 Teachers*. New York: Oxford University Press.

Maybury-Lewis, David. 1992. *Millennium: Tribal Wisdom and the Modern World*. New York: Viking.

McAleer, John. 1984. *Ralph Waldo Emerson: Days of Encounter*. Boston: Little, Brown.

McEvilley, Thomas. 2002. *The Shape of Ancient Thought: Comparative Studies in Greek and Indian Philosophies*. New York: Allworth.

McKinley, Linda, and Heather Ross. 2007. *Reflective Practice for Group Effectiveness in Human Services*. New York: Pearson.

McLeod, Ken. 2002. *Wake Up to Your Life: Discovering the Buddhist Path of Attention*. San Francisco: HarperSanFrancisco.

Merton, Thomas. 1948. *The Seven Storey Mountain*. New York: Signet Books.

Merton, Thomas. 1959. The Inner Experience. Unpublished ms.

Merton, Thomas. 1968. Asian notes. Unpublished ms.

Merton, Thomas. 1972. *New Seeds of Contemplation*. New York: New Directions.

Merton, Thomas. 1975. *The Asian Journals of Thomas Merton*. New York: New Directions.

Miller, John. 1983. *The Educational Spectrum: Orientations to Curriculum*. New York: Longman.

Miller, John. 1988. Spiritual Pilgrims. Unpublished ms.

Miller, John. 2000. *Education and the Soul: Toward a Spiritual Curriculum*. Albany, NY: SUNY Press.

Miller, John. 2006. *Educating for Wisdom and Compassion: Creating Conditions for Timeless Learning.* Thousand Oaks, CA: Corwin.

Miller, John. 2007. *The Holistic Curriculum.* Toronto: University of Toronto Press.

Miller, John. 2008. *The Journey of a Vietnam War Resistor, Narrating Transformative Learning in Education,* eds. Morgan Gardner and Ursula Kelly, 223–33. London: Palgrave Macmillan.

Miller, John. 2011. *Transcendental Learning: The Educational Legacy of Alcott, Emerson, Fuller, and Thoreau.* Charlotte, NC: Information Age Publishing.

Miller, John, and Ayako Nozawa. 2002. Meditating teachers: A qualitative study. *Journal of In-service Education* 28 (1): 179–92. http://dx.doi.org/10.1080/13674580200200201

Minott, Mark. 2010. *Reflective Teaching.* Saarbrucken: VDM Verlag.

Mitchell, Stephen, ed. 1988. *The Tao Te Ching.* New York: Harper Perennial.

Monks of New Skete. 1999. *In the Spirit of Happiness.* Boston: Little, Brown.

Moody, Raymond. 1978. *Laugh after Laugh: The Healing Power of Humor.* Headwaters Publishing.

Moody, Raymond. 1988. *The Light Beyond.* New York: Bantam.

Moon, Susan. 2010. *This Is Getting Old: Zen Thoughts on Aging with Humor and Dignity.* Boston: Shambhala.

Moore, Thomas. 1992. *Care of the Soul: A Guide for Cultivating Depth and Sacredness in Everyday Life.* New York: Walker.

Moore, Thomas. 2002. *The Soul's Religion: Cultivating a Profoundly Spiritual Way of Life.* New York: HarperCollins.

Mott, Michael. 1984. *The Seven Mountains of Thomas Merton.* Boston: Houghton Mifflin.

Murphy, Michael. 1992. *The Future of the Body: Explorations into the Further Evolution of Human Nature.* New York: Tarcher/Putnam.

Murphy, Michael, and Steve Donovan. 1999. *The Physical and Psychological Effects of Meditation.* Sausalito, CA: Institute of Noetic Sciences.

Murphy, Susan. 2006. *Upside-Down Zen: Finding the Marvelous in the Ordinary.* Boston: Wisdom.

Nachmanovitch, Stephen. 1990. *Free Play.* New York: Tarcher/Putnam.

Neihardt, John G. 2008. *Black Elk Speaks.* Albany, NY: SUNY Press.

Noddings, Nel. 2003. *Happiness and Education.* New York: Cambridge University Press. http://dx.doi.org/10.1017/CBO9780511499920

O'Donohue, John. 1999. *Eternal Echoes: Celtic Reflections on Your Yearning to Belong.* New York: Harper Perennial.

Ornish, Dean. 1990. *Dr. Dean Ornish's Program for Recovering from Heart Disease.* New York: Random House.

Pascale, Richard T., and Anthony G. Athos. 1981. *The Art of Japanese Management*. New York; Warner.

Polanyi, Michael. 1962. *Personal Knowledge: Towards a Post-Critical Philosophy*. Chicago: University of Chicago Press.

Popham, Peter. 2012. *The Lady and the Peacock: The Life of Aung San Suu Kyi*. New York: Experiment.

Poulin, Patricia A., Corey A. Mackenzie, Geoffrey Soloway, and Eric Karaoylas. 2008. Mindfulness training as an evidenced-based approach to reducing stress and promoting well-being among human services professionals. *International Journal of Health Promotion and Education* 46 (2): 72–80.

Radin, Dean. 2006. *Entangled Minds*. New York: Pocket Books.

Reagan, Timothy, Charles Case, and John Brubacher. 2000. *Becoming a Reflective Educator: How to Build a Culture of Inquiry in the Schools*. Thousand Oaks, CA: Corwin.

Richardson, Ralph. 2007. *William James: In the Maelstrom of American Modernism*. Boston: Houghton Mifflin.

Richmond, Lewis. 1999. *Work as a Spiritual Practice: A Practical Buddhist Approach to Inner Growth and Satisfaction on the Job*. New York: Broadway Books.

Rifkin, Jeremy. 1991. *Biosphere Politics*. New York: Crown.

Ross, Nancy W. 1980. *Buddhism: A Way of Life and Thought*. New York: Alfred Knopf.

Ross-Zainotz, Rebecca. 2012. Mindfulness: A Reflection on Spiritual Practice. Unpublished ms.

Ryan, Tim. 2012. *A Mindful Nation: How a Simple Practice Can Help Us Reduce Stress, Improve Performance and Recapture the American Spirit*. New York: Hay House.

Salzberg, Sharon. 1995. *Lovingkindness: The Revolutionary Art of Happiness*. Boston: Shambhala.

Samuels, Michael, and Nancy Samuels. 1975. *Seeing with the Mind's Eye: The History, Techniques and Uses of Visualization*. New York: Random House.

Savary, Louis M., and Patricia H. Berne. 1988. *Kything: The Art of Spiritual Presence*. Mahwah, NJ: Paulist Press.

Schein, E. 1973. *Professional Education*. New York: McGraw-Hill.

Schon, Donald A. 1983. *The Reflective Practitioner: How Professionals Think in Action*. New York: Basic Books.

Senge, Peter C., Otto Sharmer, Joseph Jaworski, and Betty Sue Flowers. 2004. *Presence: An Exploration of Profound Change in People, Organizations, and Society*. New York: Currency/Doubleday.

Sharon, Douglas. 1978. *Wizard of the Four Winds: A Shaman's Story*. New York: Free Press.

Sharp, Gene. 2012. *From Dictatorship to Democracy: A Conceptual Framework for Liberation*. London: Serpent's Tail.

Shoeberlein, Deborah. 2009. *Mindful Teaching and Teaching Mindfulness: A Guide for Anyone Who Teaches Anything*. Boston: Wisdom Publications.

Siegel, Daniel. 2011. The proven benefits of mindfulness. In *The Mindfulness Revolution*, ed. Barry Boyce, 136–9. Boston: Shambhala.

Singer, Jerome. 1990. *Seeing though the Visible World: Jung, Gnosis and Chaos*. New York: Harper and Row.

Smalley, Susan L., and Diana Winston. 2010. *Fully Present: The Science, Art and Practice of Mindfulness*. Cambridge, MA: DeCapo.

Smith, Huston. 1986. *The Religions of Man*. New York: Haper Perennial.

Smith, Huston. 2009. *Tales of Wonder: Adventures Chasing the Divine*. New York: Harper.

Soloway, Geoffrey B., Patricia A. Poulin, and Corey A. Mackenzie. 2010. Preparing new teachers for the full catastrophe of the 21st century classroom: Integrating mindfulness training into Initial Teacher Education. In *Breaking the Mold of Pre-Service and In-Service Teacher Education*, eds. Audrey Cohan and Andrea Honigsfeld, 219–27. Lanham, MD: R & L Education.

Steltenkamp, Michael F. 2009. *Nicholas Black Elk: Medicine Man, Missionary, Mystic*. Norman, OK: University of Oklahoma Press.

Suu Kyi, Aung San. 1997. *The Voice of Hope: Conversations with Alan Clements*. New York: Seven Stories Press.

Suzuki, Shunryu. 1970. *Zen Mind, Beginner's Mind: Informal Talks on Zen Meditation and Practice*. New York: Weatherhill.

Swedenborg, Emanuel. 1905–10. *Arcana Coelestia*. Trans. John F. Potts. New York: American Swedenborg Printing and Publishing Society.

Swedenborg, Emanuel. 1915. *The True Christian Religion*. New York: Swedenborg Foundation.

Tait, Peter Guthrie, and Balfour Stewart. 1875. *The Unseen Universe, Or Physical Speculations of a Future State*. 2nd ed. New York: Macmillan.

Talbot, Michael. 1991. *The Holographic Universe*. New York: HarperCollins.

Tan, Chade-meng. 2012. *Search Inside Yourself: Google's Guide to Enhancing Productivity, Creativity and Happiness*. New York: HarperOne.

Teilhard de Chardin, Pierre. 1965. *The Phenomenon of Man*. New York: Harper Torch Books.

Teresa of Avila. 1946. *The Collected Works*. 3 vols. Trans. E.A. Peers. London: Sheed and Ward.

Thinley, Lyonchhen Jigmi Y. 2010. Educating for Gross National Happiness. Address to Principals, Paro College of Education, Thimpu, Bhutan.

Thomsen, Robert. 1975. *Bill W.* Center City, MN: Hazelden.

Thoreau, Henry David. 1983. *Walden and Civil Disobedience*. New York: Penguin.

Thurman, Robert. 2011. Meditation and education: India, Tibet and modern America. In *Meditation in the Classroom: Contemplative Pedagogy for Religious Studies*, eds. Judith Simmer-Brown and Fran Grace, 19–20. Albany, NY: SUNY Press.

Tolle, Eckhart. 2005. *The New Earth: Awakening to Your Life's Purpose*. New York: Dutton.

Trungpa, Chogyam. 1984. *Shambhala: The Sacred Path of the Warrior*. Boston: Shambhala.

Vaughn, Francis. 1979. *Awakening Intuition*. Garden City, NY: Anchor Books.

Walsh, Roger. 1999. *Essential Spirituality*. New York: Wiley.

Wilber, Ken. 1983. *Eye to Eye: The Quest for the New Paradigm*. Garden City, NY: Anchor Books.

Willard, Christopher. 2010. *Child's Mind: Mindfulness Practices to Help Our Children Be More Focused, Calm, and Relaxed*. Berkeley, CA: Parallax Press.

Williams, Redford. 1989. *The Trusting Heart: Great News about Type A Behavior*. New York: Times Books.

Wintler, Justin. 2008. *Perfect Hostage: A Life of Aung San Suu Kyi, Burma's Prisoner of Conscience*. New York: Skyhorse.

Index